ANNUALS

ANNUALS

A COMPLETE GUIDE TO SUCCESSFUL GROWING

RICHARD BIRD

Photography by Jonathan Buckley

LORENZ BOOKS

First published in 1999 by Lorenz Books

© Anness Publishing Limited 1999

Lorenz Books is an imprint of
Anness Publishing Limited
Hermes House
88-89 Blackfriars Road
London SE1 8HA

Published in the USA by Lorenz Books, Anness Publishing Inc.,
27 West 20th Street, New York, NY 10011; (800) 354 9657

This edition distributed in Canada by Raincoast Books,
8680 Cambie Street, Vancouver, British Colombia V6P 6M9

A CIP catalogue record for this book is available from the British Library.

ISBN 1 85967 878 5

Publisher: Joanna Lorenz
Senior Editor: Caroline Davison
Copy Editor: Jackie Matthews
Designer: Ian Sandom
Production Controller: Mark Fennell
Photographer: Jonathan Buckley

Printed in Mexico

1 3 5 7 9 10 8 6 4 2

Publisher's note: In the United States, throughout the Sun Belt states, from Florida, across the Gulf Coast, south
Texas, southern deserts to Southern California and coastal regions, annuals are planted in the autumn, bloom in
the winter and spring, and die at the beginning of summer.

Half title page: *Dahlia* 'Bishop of Llandaff'.
Frontispiece top left: *Begonia semperflorens* create a colourful bed.
Frontispiece top right: French marigolds (*Tagetes patula*) line a small patio bed.
Frontispiece bottom left: The overall effect of this urn is formal without being too rigid.
Frontispiece bottom right: Wallflowers (*Erysimum*) are superb for creating
mass planting within a parterre.
Title page: Large bedding schemes are very effective but need careful planning.
Above: Miss Willmott's Ghost (*Eryngium giganteum*).
Opposite: Statice (*Limonium sinuatum*) is a classic plant for drying.

CONTENTS

INTRODUCTION

There can be few gardeners who do not grow annuals in one form or another. They are tremendously popular for many reasons, but their appeal is largely due to the fact that they flower almost instantly.

Annuals are easy to find and relatively cheap to buy. You can buy a few plants at a garden centre or nursery and within a couple of days they could be flowering in your garden, and could continue to do so throughout the summer and even well into the autumn. Alternatively, if you feel so inclined, you can have the satisfaction of growing annuals yourself from seed. This takes slightly longer than buying plants, but it is still surprisingly quick.

Annuals come in a wide range of colours, many of them very bright and brash, while others are soft and subtle. The number of ways you can use them is almost infinite. If you have the space, you can plant intricate bedding schemes, if you don't, you can have a pot on a windowsill. Another benefit of annuals is that because they last for one year only, you can try something different the next year.

This book is the perfect introduction to the range of possibilities presented by annuals and will stimulate your imagination when designing a colourful garden. It also provides plenty of practical information to enable you to achieve your goals.

Above: *Sunflowers* (Helianthus annuus*) can always be relied upon to make a dramatic statement.*

Right: *A permanent planting such as this cordyline can be underplanted with annuals.*

ANNUALS DEFINED

What is an Annual?

The definition of annuals is not quite as straightforward as it might seem at first sight. Fundamentally, annuals are plants that grow and die within one year, but in gardening terms we usually think of them as plants that we use during the course of one year only and then discard, even though they might, in certain conditions, live longer. This means that the definition also encompasses biennial plants as well as a few tender and short-lived perennials.

TRUE ANNUALS

True annuals are those that grow from seed each year, flower and then die, with only the seeds surviving to the following year. Some annuals, such as those used as bedding plants or for containers, *Lobelia* for example, have a very long season and will flower from the beginning of summer right through until the middle or end of autumn. Others, however, such as the amusingly named poached egg plant (*Limnanthes douglasii*), have a brief but dramatic flowering of perhaps only a couple of weeks or even less. In addition to length of flowering, there are also other characteristics that differentiate different types of annuals.

HARDY ANNUALS

One of the most useful types of annual, especially for use in mixed plantings, are the hardy annuals. These can be sown directly into the soil or in trays or pots to be planted out in autumn where they will survive the winter unprotected, ready to produce flowers in the late spring or early summer, well before the more tender bedding comes into flower. Forget-me-nots (*Myosotis*) are a good example of this.

HALF-HARDY ANNUALS

Half-hardy annuals will not tolerate frost and should be either grown from seed in a greenhouse or conservatory and planted out once the danger of frosts has passed or sown directly into the soil once temperatures are guaranteed to be above freezing. Those sown directly into the soil will flower much later than those that have been raised under glass in the spring and planted out as almost mature plants, and in some cases as fully mature plants in full flower. Anything grown under protection needs to be fully hardened off before it is planted outside. Examples of half-hardy annuals include French marigolds (*Tagetes patula*) and cosmos. Sometimes a distinction is made between half-hardy annuals and tender ones (see below).

TENDER ANNUALS

Tender annuals originate in tropical and sub-tropical climates and must be raised under heat in a greenhouse in order for them to flower within a year. If they were sown in the open soil after the danger of frosts had passed, they would not have a long enough season to mature and flower before the autumn frosts. The castor-oil plant (*Ricinus*) is a good example.

SOME POPULAR ANNUALS

Ageratum (floss flower)
Amaranthus caudatus (love-lies-bleeding)
Antirrhinum (snapdragon)
Calceolaria
Centaurea cyanus (cornflower)
Cosmos
Godetia
Ipomoea

Limnanthes douglasii (poached egg plant)
Myosotis (forget-me-not)
Nigella damascena (love-in-a-mist)
Papaver somniferum (opium poppy)
Petunia
Tagetes (marigold)
Tropaeolum (nasturtium)

Top: *This drift of the annual* Cleome *'Pink Queen' combines well with perennials in a mixed border. The effect of the foliage of these plants is nearly as striking as that of the flowers.*

Left: *Tender perennials are particularly good subjects for containers because they can be moved inside at the end of the season. Here a scented pelargonium, variegated fuchsia and* Persicaria captita *are displayed behind a creeping thyme.*

Right: *Brightly-coloured pelargoniums and mesembryanthemum create a spectacular display when used in this colourful bedding scheme. The scheme is unusual in that it has been created in a rock garden.*

What is a Biennial?

True annuals have a life-span of less than 12 months, and always flower within this time span. On the other hand, there are also biennials which take longer to flower. Biennials germinate in the first year, overwinter as a rosette of leaves and then flower during the following spring or summer. Occasionally biennials may be slow growing in their first year. If this is the case, the flowers may take an extra year to appear, blooming only in their third year.

TYPICAL BIENNIAL
The well-known foxglove, *Digitalis purpurea*, is a typical biennial. It is sown in the spring of the first year, either in trays or directly into the ground, and then it quickly germinates. Foxgloves grow on throughout the year with their basal leaves reaching almost full size before the start of the winter. They are fully hardy and need no winter protection. As spring of the second year approaches foxgloves grow rapidly, forming the familiar tall flower spike, which by early summer forms a statuesque spire of flowers.

SELF-SOWING
If left after flowering, foxgloves will produce copious amounts of seed which self-sow to produce another crop of plants. There are quite a number of biennials that behave in this way, which can save the gardener a lot of time. All that is required is to remove any excess or unwanted plants as well as any that have sown themselves in the wrong place.

Some plants often skip a year, the seed lying dormant then germinating the following year. *Delphinium staphisagria* and the Scotch thistle (*Onopordum acanthium*) often behave like this, but after a few years there is enough residual seed in the soil for at least some to germinate every year giving a succession of flowers every year.

DIRECT SOWING
Many biennials and some short-lived perennials that are treated as biennials, such as wallflowers (*Erysimum*) and sweet William (*Dianthus barbatus*), are sown directly into the soil. They can also be sown in trays but do better in the ground. They should be sown in shallow drills in the late spring and thinned out when they have germinated. They are left in the rows until the autumn, when they will be big enough for transferring to their final flowering positions, which will often be an area of border that has just been cleared of the current year's annuals after the flowers have faded.

SOME POPULAR BIENNIALS

Anchusa capensis (Cape forget-me-not)
Brassica oleracea (ornamental cabbage)
Campanula medium (Canterbury bells)
Delphinium staphisagria
Dianthus barbatus (sweet William)
Digitalis purpurea (foxglove)
Echium vulgare (viper's bugloss)
Eryngium giganteum (Miss Willmott's Ghost)
Erysimum, syn. *Cheiranthus* (wallflower)
Exacum affine
Glaucium flavum (horned poppy)
Hesperis matronalis (sweet rocket)
Lunaria annua (honesty)
Matthiola incana (Brompton stock)
Oenothera biennis (evening primrose)
Onopordum acanthium (Scotch thistle)
Papaver nudicaule (Iceland poppy)
Silybum marianum
Verbascum (mullein)

Left: *Biennials, such as this foxglove,* Digitalis purpurea, *usually form a rosette during their first year. After overwintering, they grow during the next spring to flower in the summer.*

Above: Eryngium giganteum, *which is also commonly known as Miss Willmott's Ghost, produces steely blue flowers and has silver, prickly foliage. It is a good flower for drying.*

Right: Lunaria annua *is, in spite of its name, a biennial. Also known as honesty, its delicate silvery seed cases are very valuable in dried flower arrangements and decorations.*

Above: Hesperis matronalis *or sweet rocket is an old-fashioned cottage garden plant that has a most delightful scent, which is especially apparent around dusk.*

What is a Tender Perennial?

Gardeners are often unaware that many of the 'annuals' they grow every year are, in fact, perennials, which in their wild state will go on flowering year after year. There are two reasons why these plants are treated as annuals in temperate regions. Some are short-lived while others are tender and would not survive a frosty winter. With care, both types could be treated as perennials, but their natures are such that it is advisable to discard the plants at the end of the year and then start afresh the following year.

SHORT-LIVED PERENNIALS

These can be typified by wallflowers (*Erysimum*), snapdragons (*Antirrhinum*) and sweet Williams (*Dianthus*

barbatus). Traditionally, these are sown afresh each year for flowering the next. However, if they are grown in soil that does not become too water-logged,

and are trimmed back after flowering, they will flower again the following year, and even the next. However, with each year the flowering becomes a little less successful and to get the best show it is best to treat them as an annual or biennial and sow each year.

Being perennial they can also be propagated vegetatively. If the sown seed produces a wallflower that has an interesting colouring, it is possible to ensure that you have it again the next year by taking cuttings from non-flowering stems. Treat these as ordinary cuttings, potting them up when they have rooted and planting out in the autumn for flowering the following year.

TENDER PERENNIALS

Different types of tender perennials are treated in various ways by gardeners. Some, including petunias, are grown exactly like annuals, which means that they are sown every year and discarded after flowering. Another group, which includes pelargoniums and fuchsias, can be propagated by cuttings in the autumn, overwintered in a greenhouse or on a windowsill, and then planted out the following spring after the danger of frosts has passed. A third group includes dahlias and tuberous begonias, and these have tubers which are simply lifted, stored in a frost-free place over the winter, and then planted out again.

SOME POPULAR TENDER PERENNIALS

Abutilon
Alonsoa warscewiczii (mask flower)
Alternanthera
Antirrhinum majus (snapdragon)
Argyranthemum
Begonia semperflorens
Bellis perennis (daisy)
Browallia speciosa
Capsicum annuum (ornamental pepper)
Celosia cristata
Chrysanthemum
Cobaea scandens (cup and saucer vine)
Coleus blumei (syn. *Solenostemon scutellarioides*)
Commelina coelestris
Coreopsis (tickseed)
Crepis rubra
Cuphea miniata
Dahlia
Eccremocarpus scandens (Chilean glory flower)
Erysimum (syn. *Cheiranthus*) *cheiri* (wallflower)
Erysimum hieraciifolium
Felicia amelloides (blue marguerite)
Gaillardia aristata (blanket flower)
Gazania
Gomphrena globosa

Helichrysum
Heliotropium arborescens (syn. *H. peruvianum*)
Hesperis matronalis (sweet rocket)
Humea elegans
Impatiens (busy Lizzie)
Limonium sinuatum
Melianthus major (honeybush)
Mimulus
Mirabilis jalapa (marvel of Peru)
Nicotiana langsdorfii
Nierembergia rivularis
Osteospermum
Pelargonium (geranium)
Polygonum capitatum (syn. *Persicaria capitata*)
Primula
Ricinus communis (castor-oil plant)
Rudbeckia hirta (coneflower)
Salvia farinacea
Senecio cineraria (syn. *S. maritima*)
Solanum pseudocapsicum (Jerusalem cherry)
Tanacetum ptarmicaeflorum
Thunbergia alata (black-eyed Susan)
Verbena × hybrida
Viola × wittrockiana (pansy)

Above: *Several salvias, including this* Salvia farinacea, *are popular 'annuals', but they are, in fact, perennials and can be overwintered in warmer areas.*

Left: *Dahlias are an ideal choice for bringing the summer to a colourful end. However, dahlias are frost tender and must be lifted and stored in a frost-free place, such as a greenhouse or conservatory, before the weather turns cold. This striking, rich orange variety is 'David Howard'.*

Right: Begonia semperflorens *will flower non-stop from early summer through to the end of autumn when it will be killed by the first frosts if it is not moved inside.*

Choosing a Scheme

Although large bedding schemes are not as popular as they once were, there is a revival of interest in the various ways that annual plants can be used and they are being appreciated anew. One of the main advantages of using annuals is their great versatility: they can be mixed with other plants or they can be used on their own.

ANNUAL VARIETY

The great thing about annuals is that they only last for one year. This may seem rather a waste, but the advantage is that once they have been planted you are not tied to a particular scheme for more than a year. If you so wish you can repeat it again the following year, but, on the other hand, you can do something completely different every year. You can simply vary the way you use the plants, that is by choosing another pattern or colour scheme, or you can use quite different plants.

THINKING AHEAD

While annuals provide summer and early autumn enjoyment in the garden, they can also be a source of much pleasure during the winter months as you plan your planting schemes for the following year. While this may simply appear to be a pleasant way of spending a winter's evening, such advance planning is very important, especially if you wish to use annuals on any scale. You need to have worked out well in advance exactly what you want to do and what you will need to achieve it. There is nothing more annoying than

devising a scheme only to discover that when you come to lay it out several plant varieties or colours are missing or you cannot get hold of them.

You can always obtain a few plants from the local garden centre or nursery, but buying in any quantity can become expensive, and you may be restricted in your choice. A much better plan, if you have time and space, is to grow your own plants. This way you can grow as many as you need (plus a few spares), and to your own satisfaction, rather than being limited to what may be second-rate plants from some other source.

INSPIRATION

Some people can invent their own schemes but many others need to look for inspiration elsewhere. Look at gardening books and magazines and visit as many gardens as you can.

Right: *Busy Lizzies* (Impatiens) *create a colourful bed that contrasts well with the surrounding green hedge. Planting in blocks of the same colour rather than mixing colours is more restful to the eye.*

Above: *This arrangement is simplicity itself. Scarlet pelargoniums with decorative leaves can be used to provide a very sophisticated display simply by growing them in terracotta pots and lining them up on top of a wall. You can, of course, use as many pots as you want.*

Above: *Annuals can be planted to create striking points of interest, as this casual display of evening primroses (*Oenothera biennis*) shows.*

Right: *Annuals are excellent plants for edging borders. Here, French marigolds (*Tagetes patula*) line a small patio bed.*

Above: *Annuals have been used here to create a large bedding scheme of subtle colouring. These bedding schemes are very effective but need a lot of careful planning.*

Informal Schemes

One of the most common ways of using bedding plants is to plant them in an informal way. Whether roughly grouped or arranged in some form of pattern, they are basically planted in a glorious mixture that is rather reminiscent of old cottage gardens. While the longer-lasting bedding plants can produce a lovely display, and are invaluable for those with limited time, you can create much more interesting effects by using some of the more unusual annuals with relatively short flowering periods, thus changing the picture as the season progresses.

DESIGN WITH CARE

Mixing plants without any real thought to their placement may well produce a riot of colour, but it can equally produce a chaotic mess. Most gardeners have probably come across examples of front gardens covered in a garish mixture of red, white, blue and orange all stirred up leaving an uncomfortable spectacle on which there is no place for the eye to rest. Take care when mixing the colours in beds and borders and try not to make the effect look too random and unplanned. Make the colours blend, the soft colours creating a restful scene, the brighter ones livening up the overall picture.

SEASONAL ANNUALS

In an informal setting, rather than the more typical bedding plants, less garish plants can often be used to create a bed that has more lasting interest. In spring, the soft colours of forget-me-nots (*Myosotis*), with foxgloves (*Digitalis*) pushing up through them and starting to flower before the forget-me-nots are over, are delightful. These

can be followed by nigellas growing around the foxgloves which in turn can be replaced by stately mulleins (*Verbascum*). Later in the season both the yellow Mexican poppy (*Argemone mexicana*) and the white (*A. grandiflora*) might add their own charm. *Crepis rubra*, a short-lived perennial, and *Silene pendula* can be used to add a soft pink note to the planting. Pale cream could also perhaps be introduced by planting *Collomia grandiflora*.

All these mixed colours will vary from week to week, creating a constantly changing, soft misty background against which splashes of eye-catching colour, perhaps the bright red of field poppies (*Papaver rhoeas*), can be added to liven it up.

Top right: *Cottage-garden simplicity and informality has been created by weaving* Collomia grandiflora *through perennials and other annuals.*

Right: *A closer shot of the above showing the way informal plantings can be random without looking too 'bitty'.*

Right: *A mixture of annuals and perennials draws the eye along a path to the front door. Here, the informality creates a wonderfully welcoming atmosphere. This contrasts well with the more formal outlines of the house. Remember that this type of gardening is not restricted to quaint cottages.*

Below: *A mass of different annuals creates the effect of a colourful meadow. Such plantings are not easy to achieve but are well worth the effort.*

Below right: *This is a semi-formal scheme in which the annuals have been beautifully planted in blocks but not to any overall pattern.*

Formal Patterns

Patterns have always played an important part in garden design, especially in the larger gardens where there was space to lay things out on a grand scale. The grand designs are now seen only in municipal plantings, especially on the coast and in parks and other public spaces. For many years they have languished, but now a new generation of gardeners has produced a revival with some very imaginative plantings. There is no reason why the gardener with only a small plot should not produce scaled-down versions of these.

STRAIGHT LINES AND SQUIGGLES

All types of patterns can be used as long as they are not so intricate that the detail is lost as the plants grow. The plot to be planted can be divided up into geometrical shapes, such as straight lines, squares, rectangles, triangles, circles and so on. An alternative is to use free-form lines and shapes that interlock or at least react with one another to produce a pleasing pattern. Scrolls and teardrops might be two examples. Each of the lines or shapes can be delineated or filled in with a different colour of flower or leaf. It is worth remembering that foliage adds a great deal to these schemes.

PICTURES

For those who want to do something special, creating a picture with flowers and foliage can be quite a challenge, and can be stunning when carried out well. At a municipal park level, one often sees the town's coat of arms (emblem) picked out in plants. Another popular theme is to make a working clock from flowers and foliage, with only the hands being made of metal or plastic. These types of designs are not only complicated and challenging but need a great deal of attention, especially with clipping, to keep them from going ragged and losing their image.

FROM PAPER TO THE BED

Patterns, especially intricate ones, need a great deal of planning and thought. They should be worked out on graph paper in the same way that you might work out an embroidery or tapestry. You should then stretch a grid, using string and canes, across the plot to be planted, corresponding to the grid on the drawing. Using the string grid as a guide to position, you can then transfer the design to the ground by outlining the shapes with sand poured from a bottle.

Right: *Although the planting in this urn is informal, the overall effect, especially with the begonias around the base, is formal, without being too rigid.*

Left: *Annuals arranged in simple geometric shapes create a satisfying rhythm along this long border. Blocks of single colours are easier on the eye than random mixes.*

Right: *With plenty of space to play with, creating a scheme like this is very gratifying. However, with a little ingenuity and good planning, there is no reason why such a scheme cannot be incorporated into a much smaller garden.*

Above: *A simple scheme using bold colours.*

Above: *A rainbow of colours can look wonderfully cheerful.*

Carpet Schemes

A long-standing tradition in public parks and gardens, carpet schemes can be used in a variety of ways. You can create intricate, formal designs, as demonstrated here, or you can use blocks of colour in bold, simple shapes, or a more informal, irregular scheme. The blocks can be created by planting out bedding plants, or you can sow directly into the soil, broadcasting different seed over each area. Striking colour contrasts can be achieved with flowers, or an interesting effect can be produced using only foliage plants. Many gardeners are under the impression that they do not have enough space for a carpet scheme, but if only small, low-growing plants are used, a very impressive design can be created in a relatively small area.

PURE BLOCKS

Carpet bedding can be arranged in some form of pattern, possibly using an edging plant in a contrasting or sympathetic colour. The blocks can be regular in shape for a formal effect or they can be more random in appearance, perhaps with their edges in a series of curves if you want to achieve a more informal look.

The edges of a block are usually clear-cut, one type of plant ends and another starts, but there is no reason why they should not merge, especially if the colours blend well. The blocks can consist purely of one colour, bright red salvias for example, or they can be a subtle or contrasting mixture. Soft blue forget-me-nots (*Myosotis*) and pink tulips may be an unoriginal combination but it is nonetheless a very effective one. If you need inspiration for devising carpet bedding schemes, look at your local park or public gardens where they are common.

WORKING IN THREE DIMENSIONS

It is worth remembering at the planning stage that different plants grow to different heights and spread, so make allowances for this. Otherwise the design may look ragged. On the other hand, it may be possible to use the different heights to advantage to create a three-dimensional bed with some areas, or even certain plants, higher than others.

PLANNING

It can be fun to work out different designs for carpet bedding schemes. For a formal scheme, you will need to draw the design on graph paper and mark out the grid on the ground using canes and string. Then draw the outline of the design on the ground by pouring sand from a bottle. If you want a less formal scheme, the sizes and shapes of the blocks of colour will be less critical and you can draw the design freehand on the ground with sand.

1 Plan the scheme and draw it on graph paper. To transfer the design to the ground, first mark out a grid using canes and string, then draw out the design using distinctively coloured sand or compost (soil mix), poured from a container. If you are using plants to mark out the design, plant these first, along the lines of sand or compost (soil mix). Complete the planting by filling in between the lines with plants, following your plan. To avoid treading on the plants as you work, use a platform. Here, ladders supported on bricks, with timber planks placed along the rungs, have been used.

2 The finished scheme illustrates the benefit of patient work. Maintenance can be carried out using the same bridging technique as was used for its construction. Maintenance consists of removing any weeds and cutting back any growth that gets too long.

Left: *A wonderfully ornate bed using many of the same plants as the detailed scheme (see below). This type of scheme can be carried out on a grand scale if space allows or devised to fit a small front garden. Much fun can be had during the winter, devising the scheme and drawing up the plans.*

Left: *The plants used in this scheme are (from the left): rows 1-3 forms of* Alternanthera; *4* Sempervivum arachnoideum; *5* Tanacetum parthenium *'Golden Moss'; 6* Senecio serpens; *7* Alternanthera; *8* Sedum spathulifolium *'Cape Blanco'; 9* Echeveria glauca; *10* Sedum spathulifolium *'Purpureum'; 11* Echeveria secunda.

Parterres

Gardeners with space to spare can create a superior bedding scheme by planting a parterre and filling it with annuals. Parterres are patterns, either geometric or free-flowing, where each element is outlined by a low hedge. Where there is enough space, patterns can become very intricate and are often best viewed from above, perhaps from the top floor of the house. However, it is possible to create a small parterre in a relatively small garden. Indeed the simplicity of such a garden and the relatively low maintenance it requires lends itself to this type of situation.

HEDGES

The only real disadvantage of this type of scheme is that you have to wait several years for the hedges to grow to the required dimensions. The best plant to use is undoubtedly box (*Buxus sempervirens*), which is, unfortunately, very slow growing. This is an advantage in that it only needs cutting once or perhaps twice a year, but it does take some years to mature. A more rapid design can be achieved by using *Teucrium chamaedrys* or the grey-leaved *Santolina pinnata neapolitana*, but both need trimming a little more frequently than box. Lavender (*Lavandula*) is more untidy but makes a very colourful and fragrant parterre.

The hedges should be about 25cm (10in) high. Prepare the ground well and be certain to remove any perennial weeds or these will cause a problem later on. Dig in plenty of organic material as the hedge is likely to be there for many years and the better the condition of the soil, the better the condition of the hedge, especially if drought conditions prevail.

THE INFILL

Make the most of the parterre and fill it with winter bedding plants as well as using it to create a colourful summer effect. Pansies are ideal for winter use. For spring, use forget-me-nots, primulas and wallflowers (*Erysimum*) as well as bulbs like tulips and narcissus.

For summer the choice is enormous. Each section of the parterre can show a different colour, or colours can be mixed. Traditional bedding plants that have a regularity in height and spread, a long flowering period and require little attention also make ideal candidates. Remember that foliage plants are excellent fillers – colourful *Coleus* (syn. *Solenostemon*), for example, or the subtle *Helichrysum petiolare*.

PERMANENCE

Since the hedges take a while to grow, the basic shapes in the parterre cannot be changed each year. This makes annuals an ideal choice for filling the beds – they will not only vary from season to season but can be completely changed from year to year.

Above: *The edges of the parterre in this walled garden are made up of box (*Buxus sempervirens*) and filled with striking* Salvia farinacea *'Victoria'*.

ANNUALS FOR FILLING A PARTERRE

Begonia semperflorens	*Heliotropium*
Bellis (daisy)	*Impatiens* (busy Lizzie)
Coleus blumei (syn.	*Lobelia erinus*
Solenostemon	*Myosotis* (forget-me-not)
scutellarioides)	*Pelargonium* (geranium)
Erysimum, syn. *Cheiranthus*,	*Primula*
cheiri (wallflower)	*Salvia patens*
Helichrysum petiolare	*Tagetes* (marigold)

Above: *Wallflowers (*Erysimum*) are superb plants for creating mass planting within a parterre. The variation in their colour establishes an overall effect, rather than the uneven one that mixing colours can often create.*

Left: *Complicated patterns, like this one with its sinuous curves, call for a simple planting, here fulfilled by using yellow pansies (*Viola × wittrockiana*).*

Mixed Borders

Annual plants do not have to be used exclusively on their own in borders or beds devoted to various types of bedding scheme. They can be mixed with other plants, perennials and shrubs. This has the advantage of vastly increasing the variety of plants that can be used in the border (enlarging the gardener's palette, in other words), as well as allowing the introduction of a variable element into what is otherwise a fixed planting. A perennial border will vary slightly from year to year as the influence of the seasons and weather alters timing and the amount of flowering, but generally this type of border will remain much the same in appearance. By using different annuals, perhaps introducing reds instead of blues, or yellows instead of white, the overall effect can be subtly altered.

CHOOSING PLANTS
Many of the popular bedding plants, such as red pelargoniums, are too rigid for the mixed border. It is better if possible to use annuals that look at home among herbaceous plants in a perennial or mixed border. Foxgloves (*Digitalis*) are ideal for early summer, and the opium poppy (*Papaver somniferum*) for later in the season. Both work well in a cottage-garden border. A more modern border with subtle colourings might include purple-leaved red orach (*Atriplex hortensis* 'Rubra') or soft blue love- in-a-mist (*Nigella damascena*). Foliage plants like *Helichrysum petiolare* add colour or act as linking themes between colours.

PERENNIAL ANNUALS
Some annuals self-sow regularly, reappearing every year without the gardener having to bother about sowing or planting them.

These work well in a mixed border where the seed can germinate and seedlings develop undisturbed, unlike in bedding areas where the soil is dug over every year, and self-sowing plants can be a nuisance. Many self-seeding plants, such as borage (*Borago officinalis*), also associate well with a herbaceous border.

PLANTING
If the annual plants are to be dotted about the border, as foxgloves might be, they can be planted directly in their positions. For a drift, however, or even a block of plants, it is preferable to dig over the area first and rejuvenate the soil with well rotted organic material. When planting, avoid setting out the plants in straight rows. An uneven number of plants makes this easier, three or five making a more satisfactory arrangement than, say, two or four. Remove the plants after flowering.

1 Remove any old plants and weeds from the area. Dig over the soil, avoiding disturbing the roots of nearby plants, and add well-rotted organic material if the soil has not been rejuvenated recently. If necessary, only dig the centre of the patch, where the plants will actually be positioned; their foliage will spread to fill the gap.

2 Feed the soil by scattering a slow-release general fertilizer, following the manufacturer's instructions.

3 Work the fertilizer into the soil using a rake. If you are going to sow seed, break the soil down to a fine tilth at the same time. For bedding plants, the soil need not be as fine – an attractive, even tilth is sufficient.

5 If you wish to use bedding plants to fill the gap, simply plant them out at the appropriate intervals to the same depths they were in their pots. Gently firm in each plant, then rake the soil to even it and to remove any footprints. Water thoroughly.

4 If you want to sow a drift of annuals, scatter the seed evenly over the ground. Rake in and water using a watering can fitted with a fine rose. If the ground is very dry, water and allow the water to drain away before sowing, then sow and water again. When the seedlings appear, thin them to the desired distance apart.

Above: *In this beautifully informal border, the annuals that have been chosen blend in perfectly with the perennials. Formal bedding plants would look completely out of place in such a planting scheme.*

Temporary Fillers

The fact that annuals only last for a year can be put to good use, not only by giving the gardener scope to vary the display from year to year but also by providing an ideal material for a temporary filler. There are two principal ways in which they can be used for this purpose: firstly to fill a whole bed for a year or two, and secondly to occupy space while the principal plants in the border are filling out.

LYING FALLOW

There are often good reasons for not planting a new permanent border in haste. It makes sense to fill in any temporary spaces between the shrubs that you have planted with annuals. Ground that has not been used for some years, for example, might harbour weed seed, both annual and perennial, and if perennials are planted any resulting weeds might be difficult to remove. By planting first with annuals, which are cleared at least once a year, the border can be easily dug over and cleaned until the weed problem has diminished.

Another good reason for taking your time when designing and planting a permanent border is that you can observe it through the seasons. You will then get firmer ideas about the types of plants you would like to plant. Rushing into buying and planting a selection of shrubs could result in having to move plants around later. This is not only a waste of your energy but you also run the risk of losing expensive ones. By adding permanent plants gradually, you can see how they look in combination, and annuals are ideal for filling the gaps until the planting is complete.

FILLING THE GAPS

After planting, herbaceous plants and shrubs may take several years to reach their ultimate size. This is particularly true of shrubs. One solution is to set the plants close together and then dig up and discard some later, but this is an expensive waste and also planting too close may cause plants to malform, for example shrubs may lose their lower branches. A far better idea is to fill in the gaps with annuals. As the main plants grow the amount of space taken up by the annuals is lessened each year until they are no longer required. This keeps the ground covered, providing less opportunity for weeds to grow and creating the impression that the border is more mature than it really is. Low annuals are unlikely to harm adjacent shrubs or perennials, allowing them to develop naturally.

PLANTING

Prepare the ground well each year before planting, removing any weeds and digging in well-rotted organic matter. Make certain that the annuals are sympathetic to the main planting: without careful selection, traditional bedding plants may look out of place.

1 When first planted a shrub border will appear almost empty as it will take some years before they grow to fill the complete border. The gaps can temporarily be filled in with annuals, using fewer and fewer each year until eventually none are required as the shrubs will have taken over completely.

2 Place the pots of plants on the area to be planted to gauge the best planting distances so that all the ground will be covered. Move them around as necessary to get the best planting effect.

3 When you are satisfied with their positions, plant each one. Dig a wide hole for each plant and set the plants so that the top of the compost (soil mix) on the root ball is level with the top of the soil. Fill around the plant with soil, firm in and then water well.

5 The plants will soon settle in and spread out to cover all the space between the shrubs. This will not only be decorative, but also act as a ground-cover, helping to keep the weeds down.

4 Tidy up around the plants, levelling the surface and removing footprints. Apply a mulch around the plants if you have enough material available.

Above: Brachycome iberidifolia, *the Swan River daisy, has been used here to fill the bare ground between shrubs. Eventually the shrubs will cover all of this space.*

Annuals as Edging Plants

Many annuals make perfect plants for edging features such as paths, borders or special beds. Paths in particular benefit from an edging. A straight path with edging on either side quickly draws the eye down along its length, and will often appear longer than it really is. Edging plants also act as a visual barrier between path and border, making the scene much neater as the bustle of the border stops at the line of edging plants. They can also be a physical barrier: if larger edging plants are used they actually stop the inner plants flopping over the path.

PLANTS TO USE
Any annuals can be used as edging plants but some look better than others in this defining role. Some, such as white alyssum, make compact plants that, when lined up along the edge of a bed or border, can be used almost like a narrow ribbon. These are best used where the other border plants gradually build up in height behind them. If tall plants are used immediately behind alyssum, then the latter is often swamped and the line is lost under a tangle of stems and foliage.

Other plants, such as bright red salvias, can be used to create a positive coloured line; it is impossible not to notice such a bright streak of colour.

Both alyssum and salvia make a very formal edge, but a plant with a looser nature, such as forget-me-not (*Myosotis*), will make a softer, much more diffuse edge to the border. It will merge gently with the plants ranged behind it so that it does not form an obvious line but rather a pretty ruffle along the edge of the border.

BLENDING
Edging is usually thought of as only one plant deep, but there is no reason why the line should not be thicker – two or even three plants deep. Avoid setting plants too far apart or the edge will look uneven. It is better to plant them fairly closely so that they blend together. This might be difficult to achieve with compact or upright plants, so choose your plants with care.

MAKING THE LINE
Planting edging is not difficult, but it is important to get the line straight or running parallel with the edge of the border or path as any deviation will show up clearly. Use a garden line or some other guide to ensure your row follows the correct line and use a measure of some sort to make certain that the plants are evenly spaced.

Right: *In this planting along the edge of a lawn, no attempt has been made to create a distinct line. Instead, poached egg plants* (Limnanthes douglasii) *create a mass of colour along the edge of the border.*

PLANTING EDGING

1 Prepare the soil thoroughly, removing any weeds and adding some well-rotted compost or soil conditioner if the soil is tired. Break the soil down to a fairly fine tilth. Set up a garden line at an even distance from the actual edge of the border. Using a standard measure, such as a length of stick, between the edge and each plant will ensure the line is even.

2 Plant the edging plants along the line at regular intervals, regulating the distance between each one with a measuring stick. Firm in each plant, rake over the soil and water. For an informal planting, you can insert a few plants behind the main row so that the edging merges into the other plants in the border.

Above: *An informal edging of* Chrysanthemum tenuiloba *'Golden Fleck' sprawls out over a path.*

Right: *Different shades of busy Lizzie (*Impatiens*) are beautifully set off by silver-leaved plants in an elaborate, formal edging.*

Above: *China pinks (*Dianthus chinensis*) make a pretty contribution to the edge of a bed or border as this vibrantly coloured variety shows.*

ANNUALS SUITABLE FOR EDGING

Ageratum (floss flower)
Begonia semperflorens
Clarkia
Crepis rubra
Dianthus chinensis (China
 pink)
Iberis amara
Lobelia

Lobularia maritima, syn.
 Alyssum maritimum
 (sweet alyssum)
Myosotis (forget-me-not)
Primula
Silene pendula
Tagetes (marigold)
Viola × wittrockiana (pansy)

Annual Climbers

We tend to think of annuals largely as temporary additions to the structure of the garden, since they only last for one year. However, there are many climbing varieties, which, although they will not continue from year to year, can put on a surprising amount of growth in one year and contribute significantly to the overall design of the garden. For example, you can add extra height and interest to a low-level border by growing annual climbers up a series of tripods (teepees).

SUPPORTS
Annual climbers can be grown up a permanent support, such as wooden trellising on a wall or in a container, or wires fixed to a wall. Alternatively, the support can be temporary, removed annually with the remains of the plant at the end of the season. Pea-sticks make excellent temporary supports, but canes or wicker pyramids are also useful.

A charming idea is to grow the annual up through a shrub. This works particularly well with shrubs that flower in the spring and perhaps look dull for the rest of the year. Once the annual starts to bloom, it will brighten up the foliage until it stops flowering. For example, grow the yellow-flowered canary creeper (*Tropaeolum peregrinum*) up through a *Spiraea* 'Arguta'.

Climbing plants can also trail, so there is no reason why many of them cannot be planted in hanging baskets and allowed to tumble down.

CULTIVATION
Climbing plants are best when they can be grown without interruption. If their growth is checked, especially by being left in the original container for too long, they will rarely grow away well. They will become weak, with yellowing leaves. Keep potting the plants on and plant them out as soon as the weather allows. Water and feed them and they will respond with vigorous growth and plenty of flowers.

Deadheading will also help the plant to produce a continuous stream of flowers. Many plants, sweet peas (*Lathyrus odoratus*) being a good example, produce shorter flowering stems as the season progresses. This is quite normal so do not think something has gone wrong.

TEMPORARY BOUNDARIES
If you are experimenting with the layout of your garden, or perhaps wish to screen off an area such as the vegetable patch, climbing annuals can make an excellent temporary boundary. A row of sweet peas, for example, can be grown up canes to create a fragrant screen, which can easily be removed at the end of the season.

Right: Ipomoea lobata *(syn.* Mina lobata*), which is also known as the cardinal climber, climbs up a metal tripod. Such plants add height to an annual border.

ANNUAL CLIMBERS

Asarina erubescens
Caiophora
Cobaea scandens (cup and saucer vine)
Convolvulus tricolor
Eccremocarpus scaber (Chilean glory flower)
Ipomoea
Lablab purpureus, syn. *Dolichos lablab*
Lathyrus odoratus (sweet pea)

Lathyrus sativus
Mikania scandens
Rhodochiton atrosanguineum
Thunbergia alata (black-eyed Susan)
Tropaeolum majus (Indian cress)
Tropaeolum peregrinum, syn. *T. canariense* (canary creeper)

Left: *Peas and beans that usually grow in the vegetable garden can be grown as decorative as well as productive plants. There are also a number of unusual varieties with different-coloured flowers and pods that are even more attractive.*

Below: Ipomoea lobata, *also known as* Mina lobata *and* Quamoclit lobata, *has masses of scarlet flowers that gradually change to orange, then fade to yellow and eventually white. When happy it will climb to 5m (16ft).*

Above: *In spite of being related to* Ipomoea lobata *(right),* I. indica *has flowers that look quite different. This is one of the morning glories, known as the blue dawn flower. It is a tender perennial and can climb up to 6m (20ft).*

Self-sowing Annuals

One of the criticisms of annuals is that they are labour intensive, because they have to be raised from seed or cuttings each year, often cosseted in heat, hardened off and then planted out. However, all this is unnecessary for self-sowing annuals, which can also be called naturalizing annuals although the term often implies that they are growing in a wild situation rather than in a border.

WORKING WITH SELF-SOWERS

Self-sowing annuals involve little work and can simply be admired. Of course, unless you inherited the annuals when you first took over the garden, you also have to sow or plant them out first. But once they have flowered for the first time, they will produce seed that drops to the ground and germinates without any interference to produce another crop of flowers next year.

You may need to thin out the seedlings if they are too thick, which is often the case as many self-sowing annuals produce copious amounts of seed. Fortunately, most annual self-sowers have heavy seed which drops around the original plants and does not colonize the whole garden. Some, however, such as busy Lizzies (*Impatiens*) and poppies (*Papaver*), use an explosive mechanism, flinging the seed far and wide. To control the level of self-sowing, pull up some plants before they seed.

Once they have finished seeding, the plants have to be removed to the compost heap. Be warned, though, any seed remaining with the plants may survive the composting process, if it does not become hot enough, and go on to colonize areas over which it is spread. Forget-me-nots (*Myosotis*) are notorious for this.

TIDYING UP

Do not be in too much of a hurry to clear up the plants once the flowers have gone over; remember to leave them long enough for the seed to set and drop. In most cases this happens even before the last flowers have appeared, but in some, *Hesperis matronalis* for example, it can take a long time after the end of flowering. In this case, if you want to tidy up, remove most of the old plants but leave a few to produce enough seed. If you want to dig over an area or renovate it and feel that you might disturb the cycle of self-sowing and germination, collect a few seeds and sow them yourself, setting the whole process in motion once more.

USING SELF-SOWERS

Surprisingly, perhaps, most of the self-sowers are very good garden plants and are well worth growing. Every garden should include at least a few of these wonderful plants. As self-perpetuating annuals they are really only suitable for the border, but as plants they can of course be used in containers, window boxes and hanging baskets. Either dig up a few plants from the border (there are usually more than enough) or sow them from seed in the usual way.

1 Most self-sowing annuals will drop their seed without need for assistance. But to ensure that seed does fall on to the soil, tap ripe seed heads to dislodge and scatter the seed before discarding the dead flowers.

2 As well as scattering the seed directly on to the ground, some can be collected by tapping the seed-head over a sheet of paper. Remove any bits of seed case or other detritus and pour the seed into a paper bag, labelled with the plant's name, until it is required. Store in a cool dry place.

THINNING SELF-SOWN ANNUALS

1 Some annuals produce copious amounts of seed that result in far too many seedlings. Overcrowding leads to drawn and starved plants, so thin out the seedlings to ensure a healthy display of full-sized flowers.

2 To remove the excess seedlings, pull them out without disturbing the roots of those plants you want to keep. If you want to transplant the seedlings elsewhere, remove them carefully using a trowel or hand fork.

3 Once you have removed all the excess plants, water the remaining ones to wash the soil down around any loosened or disturbed roots. A mulch of composted or chipped bark will help to keep the area weed-free.

SELF-SOWING ANNUALS

Adlumia fungosa (Allegheny vine)
Agrostemma (corn cockle)
Alcea rosea (hollyhock)
Angelica archangelica
Antirrhinum majus (snapdragon)
Argemone mexicana (Mexican poppy)
Atriplex hortensis 'Rubra' (red orach)
Borago officinalis (borage)
Calendula officinalis (pot marigold)
Centaurea cyanus (cornflower)
Chrysanthemum segetum
Clarkia amoena
Cosmos
Digitalis purpurea (foxglove)
Eryngium giganteum (Miss Willmott's Ghost)
Eschscholzia californica

Euphorbia lathyris
Galactites tomentosa
Hesperis matronalis (sweet rocket)
Isatis tinctoria (woad)
Limnanthes douglasii (poached egg plant)
Linaria maroccana (toadflax)
Lobularia maritima, syn. *Alyssum maritimum* (sweet alyssum)
Lunaria annua (honesty)
Myosotis (forget-me-not)
Nigella
Oenothera biennis (evening primrose)
Omphalodes linifolia
Onopordum acanthium (Scotch thistle)
Papaver somniferum (opium poppy)
Silene armeria (catchfly)
Tanacetum parthenium

Annuals for Fragrance

When choosing plants for a particular design or position there are several criteria to consider. The primary ones are flower colour, good foliage and how long the plant lasts, but fragrance, which is often overlooked, is also important. Scented flowers or foliage are an added bonus in a plant and should put it at the top of your lists.

USING FRAGRANT ANNUALS

Fragrant annuals should be grown where their scent will be appreciated most. Grow some as part of a normal border so that their perfume is enjoyed when you walk past. Grow some on the patio or next to an arbour where you sit, perhaps even eat, where the relaxing atmosphere will be enhanced by the smell of fragrant flowers. These annuals can be grown in the soil or in a container. Containers are also useful for growing annuals near to windows or doors so that the perfume will waft indoors when they are open.

Heavily scented sweet peas (*Lathyrus odoratus*) are grown by many gardeners purely for cutting for the house or for giving away as fragrant posies.

TIMING

Not all fragrant annuals are perfumed all the time. The evening primrose (*Oenothera biennis*), as its name suggests, is only fragrant during the evening. The tobacco plants, *Nicotiana alata* and *N. sylvestris* in particular, are also perfumed at this time of the day. Many annuals, as with many other types of plant, will only release their odour when the weather is warm as this is when the pollinating insects that they are trying to attract will be flying. It is not worth their while to waste energy when it is too cold.

Above: *Sweet William (*Dianthus barbatus*) are related to pinks and carnations and have their own very distinctive fragrance.*

Above: *It is the foliage of many pelargoniums that are scented rather than the flowers. These pelargonium cuttings will provide a beautifully scented display. When lightly crushed they emit an aromatic scent.*

SCENTED ANNUALS

Abronia umbellatum
Brachycome iberidifolia (Swan River daisy)
Centaurea (syn. *Amberboa*) *moschata* (sweet sultan)
Datura (syn. *Brugmansia*)
Dianthus barbatus (sweet William)
Dianthus chinensis (China pink)
Erysimum, syn. *Cheiranthus* (wallflower)
Exacum affine
Heliotropium arborescens (syn. *H. peruvianum*)

Hesperis matronalis (sweet rocket)
Lathyrus odoratus (sweet pea)
Lobularia maritima, syn. *Alyssum maritimum* (sweet alyssum)
Matthiola (stock)
Mirabilis jalapa (marvel of Peru)
Nicotiana (tobacco plant)
Oenothera (evening primrose)
Pelargonium (foliage of scented-leaved only)
Phacelia
Reseda odorata (mignonette)

Above: *Sweet peas* (Lathyrus odoratus*), one of the best-loved of all fragrant annuals, can be used as trailing plants, as here, instead of their more usual climbing habit.*

Left: *Placing scented annuals near open windows can fill the room with their fragrance. Here, the delicate scent of tobacco plants* (Nicotiana*) and heliotrope* (Heliotropium*) will waft into the house.*

Above: *The tobacco plants* (Nicotiana*) release their rich scent into the evening air and are excellent plants to use near where you sit and relax at that time of day. This one is* Nicotiana langsdorfii.

Annuals for Cutting

There is no gift more welcome when visiting than a bunch of flowers from your own garden and annuals can be ideal for making up into bouquets as well as for cutting for the house. Although not all annuals are suitable for formal arrangements, nearly all of them can be made up into bunches of one sort or another. Many of the shorter ones are useful for making little posies, and even if the flower quickly wilts, the leaves may well add something to the arrangement. Some flowers, such as sweet peas, dahlias and chrysanthemums, are grown almost exclusively to use as cut flowers, while others are used both as decoration in the borders and as the occasional cutting for the house.

Above: *Because of its pendulous habit, love-lies-bleeding (*Amaranthus caudatus*) does not strike one straight away as a plant for cutting but that very quality can make it a useful choice for flower arrangements.*

WHERE TO GROW CUT FLOWERS

It is better to allocate a special piece of ground for those flowers that are grown almost exclusively for cutting, rather than try to incorporate them into a border. The problem with growing them in a border is that every time the flowers are cut, which may be regularly, it can leave a gap. Also, the constant need for access to the plants can lead to the soil becoming compacted. Growing them in a separate plot, perhaps as part of the vegetable garden, allows much easier access for cutting as well as for tending the plants.

IN THE BORDER

While it may not be a good idea to include plants that are grown exclusively for cutting in the border, there is no reason why plants that occasionally provide a few blooms for the house cannot be incorporated. Place them in different parts of the border so that no one area is denuded after you have raided it for a bunch of flowers, and plant them where they are not too difficult to reach. Try to arrange the planting so that there are always a few flowers to cut.

GROWING CUT FLOWERS

Those plants that will be cut only occasionally can be grown in the normal manner, but those grown especially for cutting may well need special attention. They will need staking to ensure they stay upright and retain their straight stems. They will need protection against pests that may spoil the blooms: earwigs, slugs and aphids are three common pests to many plants. With many cut flowers, sweet peas (*Lathyrus odoratus*) for example, it is important to cut regularly and to remove any dead flowers as this will encourage the plant to continue producing new and reasonably sized blooms. To grow especially large blooms, it may be necessary to remove some of the buds to allow the remaining ones to develop to their full potential.

PLANTS FOR CUTTING

Agrostemma githago (corn cockle)
Amaranthus caudatus (love-lies-bleeding)
Antirrhinum majus (snapdragon)
Brachycome iberidifolia (Swan River daisy)
Calendula officinalis (pot marigold)
Callistephus chinensis (China aster)
Campanula medium (Canterbury bells)
Centaurea (syn. *Amberboa*) *moschata* (sweet sultan)
Chrysanthemum coronarium
Consolida ambigua, syn. *C. ajacis* (larkspur)
Coreopsis (tickseed)
Dianthus barbatus (sweet William)
Dianthus chinensis (China pink)
Digitalis purpurea (foxglove)
Gaillardia pulchella (blanket flower)
Gilia capitata

Godetia
Gypsophila elegans
Helianthus annuus (sunflower)
Iberis amara
Lathyrus odoratus (sweet pea)
Lavatera trimestris (tree mallow)
Limonium sinuatum
Matthiola (stock)
Moluccella laevis (bells of Ireland)
Nicotiana (tobacco plant)
Nigella damascena (love-in-a-mist)
Reseda odorata (mignonette)
Rudbeckia hirta (coneflower)
Salvia farinacea
Salpiglossis
Scabiosa atropurpurea (sweet scabious)
Tagetes erecta (African marigold)
Tagetes patula (French marigold)
Tithonia rotundifolia (Mexican sunflower)
Zinnia elegans

CUTTING ANNUALS

1 Regular cutting helps to ensure a continuing supply of new flowers. If any of the flowers are allowed to run to seed, vital energy that would otherwise be channelled into producing new blooms is used up. Removing dead flowers and any developing seed helps to conserve this energy.

2 The best time to cut flowers is just as they are opening or about to open. Cut the longest available stalk, which can be trimmed back later if necessary. Plunge the cut flowers up to their necks in lukewarm water and store them in a cool shady place for a few hours before you arrange them in a vase or jug.

3 The length of time that a cut flower stays fresh and attractive varies from variety to variety. This period can be extended by adding a proprietary cut-flower food to the water at the dosage recommended on the packet.

4 Before placing in a vase cut the stems to the required length and remove all leaves that would be below water when arranged. The style of the arrangement is up to you – experiment with different combinations, and use your imagination!

5 The finished vase will make the effort of raising and growing the plants worth while. The best place for cut flowers is in a cool, airy position away from direct sunlight.

Above: *Dahlias make excellent cut flowers and can be grown in a general border, as here, or in a separate plot, especially for cutting. This variety is 'Aylett's Gaiety'.*

Annuals for Drying

Drying annuals prolongs their useful life, allowing them to be used as decoration for a second year or even longer. (Do not keep them too long, though; there is nothing sadder than faded, dusty dried flowers.) A number of annuals are grown specifically for drying, but it is surprising how many ordinary annuals can also be effectively dried. As well as display, many can be used as components of a pot-pourri, either for their colour or their fragrance.

GROWING FOR DRYING

Annuals that are grown specifically for drying are probably best grown in separate rows, especially if they are needed in quantity. Those that are used to just add a bit of variety to an arrangement and therefore are needed in small quantities only can be grown in ordinary borders.

DRYING

There are several different ways in which to dry annuals, but air-drying is the simplest, the cheapest and in many ways the most effective.

The best time for harvesting flowers for drying is on a dry day after any early morning dew or overnight rain has evaporated. The exact time that a flower needs to be picked varies from variety to variety, but generally the best time is soon after it has opened, or in some cases while it is still in bud. You might like to include some buds in your final dried-flower arrangement.

Cut the stems cleanly with a pair of secateurs (pruners), leaving as long a stem as possible. Strip off the lower foliage, leaving bare stems. Place the stems in small bunches and bind them with rubber bands, raffia or string. The advantage of rubber bands is that they contract to take up the shrinkage that takes place as the stems dry. If carelessly tied with string the bunch may come loose, scattering the flowers and possibly damaging them.

Hang the bunches upside down in a warm, airy place. Avoid hanging them where they are in direct sunlight or anywhere where the air is liable to be damp. The ideal place is in a warm kitchen, away from any steaming kettles or pans. As well as being practical, drying flowers in the kitchen can also be very decorative. An airing cupboard is another perfect place.

The flowers are ready to use when they are completely dried. Check the thickest part of the flower or stem, breaking one if necessary to test it.

Individual flowers for use on home-made greetings cards or bookmarks for giving as gifts can be dried by pressing with a heavy weight between sheets of blotting paper or by burying them in silica gel crystals.

Right: *Cornflowers* (Centaurea cyanus) *are valuable as they add the colour blue to the dried-flower arranger's palette.*

FLOWERS FOR DRYING

Ageratum (floss flower)
Amaranthus caudatus (love-lies-bleeding)
Ammobium alatum
Atriplex hortensis
Briza maxima (greater quaking grass)
Briza minor (lesser quaking grass)
Calendula officinalis (pot marigold)
Celosia argentea
Celosia cristata
Centaurea cyanus (cornflower)
Centaurea (syn. *Amberboa*) *moschata* (sweet sultan)
Clarkia
Consolida ambigua, syn. *C. ajacis* (larkspur)
Gilia capitata
Gomphrena globosa
Gypsophila elegans
Helichrysum bracteatum, syn. *Bracteantha bracteata* (everlasting flower)
Helipterum roseum (syn. *Acroclinium roseum*)
Hordeum jubatum (squirrel tail grass)
Lagurus ovatus (hare's-tail grass)
Limonium sinuatum
Lunaria annua (honesty)
Moluccella laevis (bells of Ireland)
Nicandra physalodes (apple of Peru, shoo-fly)
Nigella damascena (love-in-a-mist)
Onopordum acanthium (Scotch thistle)
Salvia horminum (syn. *S. viridis*)
Scabiosa atropurpurea (sweet scabious)
Setaria italica (foxtail millet, Italian millet)
Stipa pennata
Tagetes erecta (African marigold)

Above: *Pot marigolds (Calendula officinalis) tend to shrivel slightly when dried but are good because of their strong orange colour.*

Right: *The bells of Ireland (Moluccella laevis) dry to a pale green that soon changes to soft cream.*

Above: Limonium sinuatum *is one of the classic plants for drying. It can be grown, as here, as part of a border, but is often grown separately, especially for cutting and drying.*

FLOWERS AND FOLIAGE

Finding the Right Annual

There is a tremendous range of colours in annual plants, so wide that with a little thought and imagination you can paint any picture you like.

USING COLOURS

Each colour has many tones and shades, and annuals reflect all the possible nuances. On the whole, though, most annuals are of a bright nature and this must be taken into account when using them.

Since so many annuals come from hot, Mediterranean-type climates, they often have bright colours, which are necessary in harsh, bright light for attracting passing pollinators. Many gardeners take advantage of this, using annuals to provide strong impact in the garden. A sudden splash of bright red pelargoniums or salvias, for example, will always catch the eye. However, bright colours are not always easy to combine as they may clash with one another or create a confused picture in which there is nowhere for the eye to rest. Hot, vibrant colours can get lost in the hurly-burly of a mixed border and tend to look better when used as part of a design for bedding plants. They can look even better when used to enliven the façade of a building, possibly in window boxes or hanging baskets. This is where bright pelargoniums and trailing petunias come into their own.

Many annuals, nonetheless, are subtly coloured and can be combined to create a more romantic image. The misty blues of love-in-a-mist (*Nigella damascena*), the soft, silky pinks of lavateras, the smoky lavenders of some of the opium poppies (*Papaver somniferum*), or the apricots of *Collomia grandiflora* can be used singly in drifts or combined to form a restful image.

COMBINING COLOURS

Some colours mix better than others. Near neighbours on the artist's colour wheel combine together much more sympathetically than the contrasting colours that are opposite each other. Thus, red flowers merge seamlessly with purple ones, but orange will stand out quite starkly against blue. Combining colours can be used to great effect, but try to avoid creating a restless image as a result of combining too many colours at once. Drifts of colour are much easier on the eye.

When you grow plants from seed you can use particular colour strains which are almost guaranteed to come true. However, if you buy mixed seed, the plants could turn out to be any colour and this must be borne in mind when planting them out. Similarly, when you buy seedlings from a garden centre or nursery it may be a good idea to see at least some in flower before you buy to ensure you get what you want. Your carefully planned scheme could be ruined by a wishy-washy pink appearing where you expected a strong yellow.

Left: *A lot of careful thought needs to be given to colourful bedding schemes like this. Drawing them out on a piece of graph paper with coloured pencils helps with planning – it can be an enjoyable way to pass a winter evening.*

Above: *Foliage plays an important part in any colour scheme. Here the delicate pink of this opium poppy* (Papaver somniferum*) is beautifully set off against the grey leaves.*

Above: *Sweet peas* (Lathyrus odoratus*) come in a wide range of colours and can be mixed, as here, or grown separately.*

Left: *One of the benefits of modern breeding methods is the consistency in colour that can be produced. Here the French marigold,* Tagetes patula *'Aurora Primrose', produces a batch of identical flowers.*

Red

Red has two faces: one is tinged with orange and the other with blue. The orange reds are hot colours and combine well with oranges and golden and orange yellows. On the other hand, the blue reds are more subdued but often richer, more velvety in tone and combine well with purples, violets and blues. The flame reds are exciting, while the blue reds are more sophisticated.

ORANGE REDS

Although there are times when the two groups of red can be used together, they generally do not mix in a pleasing way and so tend to be kept separate. Use orange reds where you want to inject some vibrancy and excitement into your garden designs, whether it be in beds and borders or in hanging baskets and other containers. But remember that, like parties, too much of a good thing can become monotonous after a while. Use hot strong colours sparingly, but when you do, make them tell.

Hot reds have the advantage of appearing to draw nearer than they really are, and show up well at a distance. This is one of the reasons why they are so good on the façades of buildings. For example, even a single geranium will stand out in a window box on a third-floor windowsill. A pale lavender flower would be invisible.

BLUE REDS

Blue reds can be used more extensively than orange reds as they are less intense. Unfortunately, as far as annuals are concerned plant breeders obviously feel that gardeners prefer the hot, flame reds as these are by far in the majority. However, purple reds now seem to be amongst the most popular colours of the trailing petunias, and hanging baskets filled with these seem to add a touch of richness to a building.

Below: *Reds can vary in their intensity but this* Verbena *'Sandy Scarlet' is as intense and brightly coloured as they come – it is positively dazzling and makes a great contribution to any bed.*

POPULAR RED ANNUALS

Adonis aestivalis	*Lathyrus odoratus* 'Winston
Alcea rosea 'Scarlet'	Churchill'
Amaranthus caudatus (love-	*Linum grandiflorum*
lies-bleeding)	*Lobelia erinus* 'Red Cascade'
Antirrhinum 'Scarlet Giant'	*Lobelia erinus* 'Rosamund'
(snapdragon)	*Malope trifida* 'Vulcan'
Begonia semperflorens	*Nicotiana* 'Crimson'
'Lucifer'	*Papaver rhoeas* (field poppy)
Begonia semperflorens	*Pelargonium* (many red
'Volcano'	varieties)
Cleome spinosa (syn. *C.*	*Petunia* 'Mirage Velvet'
hassleriana) 'Cherry	*Petunia* 'Red Star'
Queen'	*Petunia* 'Scarlet'
Cosmos bipinnatus 'Pied	*Salvia splendens*
Piper Red'	*Tagetes patula* 'Cinnabar'
Dianthus chinensis 'Fire	*Tagetes patula* 'Red Marietta'
Carpet'	*Tagetes patula* 'Scarlet
Impatiens (busy Lizzie)	Sophie'
Impact Scarlet	*Tropaeolum majus* 'Empress
Impatiens 'Super Elfin Red'	of India'
Impatiens 'Tempo Burgundy'	*Verbena* 'Blaze'
Impatiens 'Tempo Scarlet'	*Verbena* 'Defiance'
Lathyrus odoratus	*Verbena* 'Sandy Scarlet'
'Airwarden'	*Verbena* 'Sparkle'

Above: *Dahlias produce some very rich reds indeed, but few are as vivid as this 'Bishop of Llandaff' with its flame-red flowers.*

Above: *Pelargoniums are available in a wide range of striking reds, varying from orange red, through scarlet to crimson as well as the more purple reds.*

Right: *A plant that produces consistently good red flowers is the busy Lizzie (Impatiens). It is a valuable low-growing plant for painting swathes of red in a bedding sheme.*

Pink

Pink is a very useful colour in the annual spectrum. It is obviously not as bright as the reds but it can still be quite bright and even startling and brash, particularly when mixed with a tinge of purple and moving more towards cerise and magenta shades. On the other hand pink can be very soft and romantic. You have to be careful in choosing the right colour for the effect you want to get. If possible see the plant in flower first.

USING PINK

Generally, pinks are considered soft colours and are mixed with similar tones. They tend to mix best with lavenders and soft blues. But they can be used with reds to tone them down a bit. Pinks do not mix harmoniously with bright yellows and oranges.

Pink-coloured annuals can be used in a wide range of garden situations, from hanging baskets and window boxes to bedding schemes or perhaps mixed in with perennials. They look particularly good in containers, especially stone or stone-coloured ones.

POPULAR PINK ANNUALS

Agrostemma githago 'Milas'
Alcea rosea 'Rose'
Antirrhinum majus (snapdragon – numerous pink varieties)
Argyranthemum (syn. *Chrysanthemum*) *frutescens* 'Mary Wootton'
Begonia semperflorens 'Pink Avalanche'
Callistephus chinensis (China aster)
Centaurea cyanus (cornflower – pink forms)
Crepis rubra
Dianthus (carnation, pink – various varieties)
Diascia (numerous varieties)
Godetia grandiflora 'Satin Pink'
Helichrysum bracteatum (syn. *Bracteantha bracteata*) 'Rose'
Helipterum roseum (syn. *Acroclinium roseum*)
Impatiens (busy Lizzie) 'Impact Rose'
Impatiens 'Super Elfin Rose'
Impatiens 'Tempo Blush'
Lathyrus odoratus (sweet pea – numerous pink varieties)
Lavatera trimestris 'Mont Rose'
Lavatera trimestris 'Pink Beauty'
Lavatera trimestris 'Silver Cup'
Malope trifida 'Pink Queen'
Matthiola (stock – numerous varieties)
Nicotiana 'Domino Salmon-Pink'
Nigella damascena 'Miss Jekyll Pink'
Papaver somniferum (opium poppy)
Pelargonium (many pink varieties)
Petunia (numerous pink varieties)
Silene coeli-rosa 'Rose Angel'
Silene pendula 'Peach Blossom'
Verbena 'Amour Light Pink'

Above: *This is a spectacular mass planting of* Osteospermum *'Lady Leitrim', whose flowers grow pinker as they age. They create an informal meadow-like effect planted in this way.*

Above: *There is really nothing to surpass the delicate paper-tissue flowers of the opium poppy* (Papaver somniferum) *– it produces some of the most soft and subtle pinks for the annual border.*

Above: Oenothera speciosa *'Rosea' produces a profusion of delicate pink flowers. The species form,* O. speciosa, *known as white evening primrose, has white flowers that turn pink as they age, creating a delightful effect.*

Above: *Foxgloves (*Digitalis*) create wonderfully elegant spires of flowers, bringing height to a planting scheme. These flowers vary in colour from a light pink to purple and look very statuesque in the border.*

Left: Cleome spinosa (*syn.* C. hassleriana) *looks like a firework sending off sparks in all directions. The flower buds are dark pink, fading as they open.*

Above: *Cosmos flowers over a long period and comes in a wide range of colours. There are several pinks including this lovely dark one, 'Versailles Tetra'.*

Blue and Lavender

Blue can be that bright, clean-cut colour that has a great intensity or it can be softened to such an extent that it only has a whisper of colour left, creating a very soft, hazy image. Intense blues can be used in a bold way in the garden, but the softer blues are good for romantic container arrangements, especially those in large stone pots or urns.

USING BLUES

Blues are versatile and can be combined with most colours. They create a rather rich, luxurious combination with purple reds, but avoid mixing them with orange reds. With orange, however, the effects can be startling, so use this combination sparingly, otherwise it becomes overpowering and rather tedious to look at.

Blue and yellow is another exciting combination. These colours, which are near opposites on the artist's colour wheel, form a fresh, clean-looking contrast. Pale blues and yellows are more hazy and have a softer, more romantic image, but still retain a distinctive fresh quality, much more distinct than, say, soft blues and pinks.

Lavenders combined with pinks are a wonderfully romantic combination. Although they can look washed out in bright light, they can look wonderful in a grey, northern atmosphere. Blues set against silver or grey foliage create an interesting combination that is severe yet soft.

*Right: The beautifully intricate annual love-in-a-mist (*Nigella damascena*) is typically a delicate light blue. However, love-in-a-mist is now available in a wider range of colours including dark blue. The impact of the blue petals is further enhanced by the elegant ruff of green filigree foliage.*

POPULAR BLUE AND LAVENDER ANNUALS	
Ageratum houstonianum	*Lathyrus odoratus* (sweet
Borago officinalis (borage)	pea – various varieties)
Brachycome iberidifolia	*Limonium sinuatum* 'Azure'
(Swan River daisy)	*Limonium sinuatum* 'Blue
Campanula medium	Bonnet'
(Canterbury bells)	*Lobelia erinus*
Centaurea cyanus	*Myosotis* (forget-me-not)
(cornflower)	*Nemophila menziesii* (baby
Consolida ambigua, syn. *C.*	blue-eyes)
ajacis (larkspur)	*Nigella damascena* (love-in-a-
Cynoglossum amabile	mist)
Echium 'Blue Bedder'	*Nigella hispanica*
Echium vulgare	*Nolana paradoxa* 'Blue Bird'
Felicia bergeriana (kingfisher	*Petunia* (some varieties)
daisy)	*Primula* (blue varieties)
Gilia	*Salvia farinacea* 'Victoria'

Above: *The flowers of the Californian bluebell (*Nemophila menziesii*) shade from blue to white in the centre, which makes them a useful two-tone bedding plant.*

Above: *The pink buds and blue flowers of the intriguingly named biennial viper's bugloss (*Echium vulgare*) make this a spectacular plant for the mixed border.*

Above: *The highly architectural shoo-fly plant (*Nicandra physalodes*) can be used as a specimen plant or in mass plantings.*

Above: *Lobelia is available in a range of blues and is valuable for the solid mass of colour it produces and the length of its flowering period.*

Purple and Violet

Purple and violet are borderline between blue and red: purple is red with a dash of blue while violet is blue with a dash of red. Purple has a richness about it, which is why it has always been a sign of luxury and class. It is a strong colour – paler shades would be described as mauve. Similarly, violet is a deep colour, with lighter forms becoming mauves or lilacs.

USING PURPLE

Purple is a solid colour, because of its depth, and a patch of it always appears as a strong block of colour, never as a misty haze. However, the over-use of purple can have a deadening effect, creating a rather leaden appearance. A hanging basket of purple petunias can look stunning, but ten such baskets hung in close proximity lose all their impact and can be positively dull. As purple tends to sink back into green foliage, making it even more difficult to see, contrast it with silver or grey foliage for a better effect.

While purple is a sombre colour, violet is a more lively one, and has still more vibrancy when on the dark side. While it is less leaden than purple, it should still be used with care and discretion.

Both purple and violet can be used more extensively if they are mixed with other colours. Lighter colours, such as yellows and whites, contrast with and stand out against purple. Purple also harmonizes well with purple reds and purple blues, but if these are too dark, the colours tend to blend too much, creating a leaden effect. Lime-green flowers such as lime zinnias and the foliage of *Helichrysum petiolare* 'Limelight' make excellent companions. These are colours that need to be experimented with to some degree. Try a range of different combinations until you find something that you are pleased with, but do not always expect everybody to agree with your choice of colours.

Left: *The deep purple flowers of honesty (*Lunaria annua*) have a luminous quality that looks attractive both in the evening light and also in the gloom of a woodland or other shady setting.*

Right: Silene armeria *'Electra' is a good bedding plant, forming a sheet of magenta-purple flowers for a short season in the summer.*

Above: *The delightful* Galactites tomentosa *is a non-troublesome thistle that produces light purple flowers. These look wonderfully striking against the variegated foliage. This is a particularly good plant for including in the mixed border.*

Above right: *Ageratums make perfect bedding plants with their small powder-puff flower heads that last throughout the summer and well into the autumn. This rich reddish-purple variety is 'North Star'.*

Right: Brachycome iberidifolia, *the Swan River daisy, comes in a variety of shades that range from blue to violet and even include rich purple.*

White and Cream

White flowers are very fashionable. Long associated with purity, peace and tranquillity, they are much in demand for wedding bouquets and as cut flowers. The purity and clarity of white gives it a touch of class and sophistication that other colours can rarely match. Cream is white with a little yellow added. It is a more sensuous, luxurious colour, and lacks the more clinical qualities of pure white.

USING WHITE

White is a good colour for brightening up a planting scheme or container display and can be used to illuminate dark corners of the garden. White busy Lizzies, for example, in a hanging basket against a dark background or in shade will shine out. White also has a magical quality as the light fades in the evening, standing out long after other colours have disappeared in the gloom. This makes it an excellent choice for use in containers and other displays, especially in areas where you sit in the evening.

White will mix well with other colours, although it can sometimes be a little too stark in contrast with some. Cream will often blend in more sympathetically, especially with colours on the orange-red side of the colour spectrum.

One big drawback with white flowers is that they so often refuse to die gracefully. Once they have finished flowering you are left with shrivelled brown petals that stand out far too well against the remaining white flowers. To keep such displays at their best, it is essential to deadhead at least once a day.

POPULAR WHITE AND CREAM ANNUALS

Alcea rosea (hollyhock – white varieties)
Antirrhinum 'White Wonder'
Argyranthemum (syn. *Chrysanthemum*) *frutescens* (white varieties)
Centaurea (syn. *Amberboa*) *moschata* 'The Bride' (sweet sultan)
Clarkia pulchella 'Snowflake'
Cleome spinosa (syn. *C. hassleriana*) 'Helen Campbell'
Consolida ambigua (syn. *C. ajacis*) 'Imperial White King'
Cosmos bipinnatus 'Purity'
Dianthus (carnation, pink – various varieties)
Digitalis purpurea alba (white foxglove)
Eschscholzia californica 'Milky White'
Eustoma grandiflorum (white varieties)
Gypsophila elegans 'Giant White'
Helianthus annuus 'Italian White'
Helichrysum bracteatum (syn. *Bracteantha bracteata*) 'White'
Hibiscus trionum (flower-of-the-hour)
Iberis amara
Impatiens (busy Lizzie) Super Elfin White
Lathyrus odoratus (sweet pea – various varieties)
Lavatera trimestris 'Mont Blanc'
Limonium sinuatum 'Iceberg'
Lobelia erinus 'Snowball'
Lobularia maritima, syn. *Alyssum maritimum* (sweet sultan)
Malope trifida 'Alba'
Matthiola (stock – white varieties)
Nemesia 'Mello White'
Nemophila maculata
Nicotiana alata, syn. *N. affinis* (tobacco plant)
Nicotiana sylvestris
Nolana paradoxa 'Snowbird'
Omphalodes linifolia
Osteospermum 'Glistening White'
Papaver somniferum (opium poppy – white varieties)
Pelargonium (various white forms)
Petunia (various white forms)
Tripleurospermum inodora 'Bridal Robe'
Viola × wittrockiana (pansy – white varieties)

Left: *The tender perennial* Osteospermum *'Prostratum' is a lovely pure white, but it needs plenty of sun, as the flowers only open in sunlight.*

Right: *Cream is a good colour to combine with a wide range of other colours, especially schemes planted with hot yellows and orange reds. The marigold* Tagetes *'French Vanilla' demonstrates clearly the true beauty of this colour.*

Above: Iberis crenata *is rather more lax than other species of candytuft, and produces an abundance of stunning white flowers. These emerge from the mauve buds that are still held in the centre of the flower head.*

Above: *Many flowers also have white forms including this foxglove,* Digitalis purpurea alba.

Above: *For ethereal, billowing clouds of white flowers it is hard to beat* Gypsophila, *which brings an elegant tracery to a planting scheme. This annual form is* G. elegans *'White Elephant'.*

Above: *The old-fashioned annual* Collomia grandiflora *produces beautiful flowers at the height of summer that are the most wonderful peach-cream colour.*

Yellow and Gold

There are three distinct colours within the yellow part of the artist's colour spectrum, all exhibiting different qualities in a planting scheme. One side is tinged with green and may be described as a cool colour, while the other side is tinged with orange, making it very much a hot colour. In between are the pure, clear yellows. The orange yellows as well as pure gold have a warm, cosy feeling about them, whereas the greener yellows are much fresher and cleaner looking. The pure, clear yellows make a tremendous impact and attract the eye more readily than most other colours. Yellow is also a stimulating colour. For this reason, yellow flowers are often planted in gardens outside hospices where people come for healing.

POPULAR YELLOW AND GOLD ANNUALS

Alcea rosea 'Yellow'
Anoda cristata 'Buttercup'
Antirrhinum majus (snapdragon – yellow varieties)
Argemone mexicana (Mexican poppy)
Argyranthemum (syn. *Chrysanthemum*) *frutescens* 'Jamaica Primrose'
Calendula officinalis 'Kablouna'
Chrysanthemum segetum
Coreopsis 'Sunray'
Glaucium flavum (horned poppy)
Helianthus annuus (sunflower)
Limnanthes douglasii (poached egg plant)
Limonium sinuatum 'Goldcoast'
Lonas annua
Mentzelia lindleyi
Mimulus (creeping zinnia – various varieties)
Sanvitalia procumbens
Tagetes (marigold – yellow varieties)
Tropaeolum majus (Indian cress)
Tropaeolum peregrinum, syn. *T. canariense* (canary creeper)
Viola × wittrockiana (pansy – yellow varieties)

USING YELLOWS

The three colours are often used indiscriminately, yet with a bit of care would fit in with their companions far more comfortably. Clear yellow will sit happily with most other colours, purple being the least comfortable combination, although even this contrast can be worthwhile if not overdone.

A bed or container of warm yellows is always welcoming. These cheerful colours go well with flame reds, oranges, creams and buffs, but they can dominate their companions.

The green or lemon yellows look much better when associated with greens, blues and white. They can be gay and bright, but create a fresher effect than the warmer colours.

Right: *The poached egg plant* (Limnanthes douglasii) *is much-loved for its cheerful disposition as well as its ability to self-sow and reappear each year.*

Above: *A self-sowing wallflower that reappears every year without any intervention from the gardener is the delightful* Erysimum helveticum.

Above: *For sheer architectural grandeur there is little to beat the giant spires of mulleins* (Verbascum) *which tower 2m (7ft) or more above the border.*

Above: *Marigolds come in an infinite range of yellows, golds and oranges and even reddy browns. This one is a French marigold called* Tagetes patula *'Golden Gem'.*

Above: *Charming argyranthemums with their daisy-like flowers come in pink and white as well as yellow. Here the golden yellow is set off brilliantly by the dark green of the foliage.*

Above: *Annual chrysanthemums are perhaps not as showy as their perennial cousins, but they can still put on a wonderful display. This one is called* Chrysanthemum tenuiloba *'Golden Fleck'.*

Orange

Orange is a warm, friendly colour. It is predominantly a colour of late summer and autumn, but it is welcome at any time of the year. It has quite a wide range of shades, from deep gold (the lighter golds are closer to yellow) through to almost flame red. At the deeper end of the spectrum, it is a hot colour, exciting and vibrant. At the golden end it is warm rather than hot and can be used a bit more freely.

USING ORANGE

Orange mixes well with most colours although the redder shades are not so complementary with the bluer reds, including purple and pink, unless you like to combine colours that clash. The more yellow colours mix better with blues.

Orange shows up well against green foliage and can be picked out at a distance. It can be used wherever annuals are appropriate and is frequently found in the form of African marigolds (*Tagetes erecta*) and French marigolds (*T. patula*), in large bedding schemes.

Although orange is most widely seen in autumn gardens, not only in flowers such as chrysanthemums but in trees and shrubs with coloured foliage and berries, there are also many annuals that can add a vibrant orange note throughout the year. The winter-flowering pansies (*Viola × wittrockiana* Universal Series) include orange varieties which continue flowering into the spring, and wallflowers (*Erysimum*), snapdragons

Right: Although osteospermums have the annoying habit of closing up on dull days, they can still make a splash with their bright colours. This pure orange variety is O. hyoseroides *'Gaiety'.*

(*Antirrhinum*) and pot marigolds (*Calendula*) then come into their own, the latter often flowering quite early if it has been left to self-sow. During the summer, nasturtiums (*Tropaeolum*) in various shades will follow.

POPULAR ORANGE ANNUALS

Alonsoa warscewiczii (mask flower)
Antirrhinum majus (snapdragon – various varieties)
Calceolaria (various varieties)
Calendula officinalis (pot marigold – various varieties)
Emilia coccinea, syn. *E. flammea* (tassel flower)
Erysimum (syn. *Cheiranthus*) *cheiri* 'Fire King'
Erysimum (syn. *Cheiranthus*) *cheiri* 'Orange Bedder'
Eschscholzia californica
Helichrysum bracteatum, syn. *Bracteantha bracteata* (various varieties)
Impatiens (busy Lizzie) Impact Orange
Impatiens 'Mega Orange Star'
Mimulus (creeping zinnia – various varieties)
Nemesia 'Orange Prince'
Rudbeckia hirta (coneflower – various varieties)
Tagetes erecta (African marigold – various varieties)
Tagetes patula (French marigold – various varieties)
Tithonia rotundifolia 'Torch'
Tropaeolum majus (Indian cress – various varieties)
Viola × wittrockiana (pansy – various varieties)
Zinnia (various varieties)

Above: *Cannas can be used to make strong extrovert statements in a bedding scheme. Many have bright orange flowers and this one, 'Roi Humbert', has contrasting purple foliage as an added bonus.*

Above: *Calceolarias have curious slipper-shaped flowers. The bedding varieties come in shades of yellow, orange or red. This bright orange variety is 'Kentish Hero'.*

Mixed Annuals

The flowers of many annuals are not, of course, restricted to a single colour. Each flower may consist of several colours although there may be one basic colour. For example, salpiglossis have dark or differently coloured throats and very prominent veining, which help to disguise or alter the overall appearance of the base colour. This means that flowers that are basically coloured orange will have quite a different effect in a display than totally orange flowers, such as calendula.

USING MIXED COLOURS

Some plants have several colours in their flowers, without any one being dominant, and planning precise colour schemes with this type of flower is very difficult if you are not to avoid a chaotic mixture. This is not to say that they are not worth growing, simply that they have to be handled differently and rather carefully. You must decide what their overall effect is likely to be when used in a specific planting scheme. You should also be careful when mixing them with other plants that have mixed colours as the general effect may become rather uneven and restless. Sometimes it can be effective to echo one of the colours in an adjacent planting.

There is an increasing tendency on the part of seed merchants to market packets of mixed colours rather than just a single one. For instance, some merchants may only have mixed colours of snapdragon (*Antirrhinum*) available. You can sometimes achieve a lovely cottage-garden effect with these mixtures, for example of sweet peas, but if you do want a more planned scheme, check in different catalogues and with

luck you should find the specific colours you want. Surprisingly, it is often the smaller companies that offer a better service in this respect.

A similar problem arises when buying plants from a garden centre or nursery. Sometimes it can be impossible to find the colour you want and you have to make do with a mixture. At other times the packs of plants may not be labelled. Although it is not always a good idea to wait for annuals to flower before buying, it may sometimes be necessary to ensure that you get the right colours.

If you save your own seed, of snapdragons for example, there is no guarantee that the resulting seedlings will be the same colour as the parent from which the seed was collected. This is further complicated by the fact that some plants are more likely to come true than others.

Right: *These marigolds (*Tagetes*) are two-toned but the colours are relatively close to each other on the colour wheel and so they blend well together giving a harmonious effect.*

Above: *Many flowers change colour as the flowers mature and finally fade. This* Verbena *'Peaches and Cream' goes through several stages.*

Below: *A common coloration is where one colour shades into another. In this pelargonium the dark pink merges into a much softer one.*

Above: *Where two colours are strongly contrasted, as in this nemesia, the overall effect is much more startling and eye-catching.*

Annuals for Foliage

There is a tendency to think of annuals only in terms of their flower-power, but they have a lot more to offer. Indeed, many are useful solely for their foliage, which can be wonderfully coloured, but there are a few that are notable for both their foliage and their flowers. Even plain green foliage often comes in attractive and interesting shapes, setting off the flowers very effectively.

FOLIAGE COLOUR

In annuals, foliage colours are far from being restricted to green. Red orach (*Atriplex hortensis* 'Rubra') has rich purple leaves which go well with pinks and silvers, and it is a marvellous plant for dotting about a mixed border of soft colours. Several silver-foliaged annuals, which are particularly good for setting off blues and pinks, can be used as part of a formal bedding scheme or in a more mixed planting. The statuesque Scotch thistles (*Onopordum acanthium*) are too big for most bedding schemes but they fit well into large borders or stand as individual plants.

As well as these striking single colours, there are some annuals with variegated foliage: *Euphorbia marginata* has a cool white and green combination, while the tender shrub *Abutilon megapotamicum* 'Variegatum' has dark green leaves liberally splashed with gold. *Coleus* (syn. *Solenostemon*), in particular, comes in a wide range of colours and markings, and will often outshine a display of flowers.

OTHER QUALITIES

The shapes of leaves are also of value. The castor-oil plant (*Ricinus communis*), with its large-fingered leaves, for example, is very eye-catching.

The grey or silver leaves of melianthus are also very architecturally shaped.

Scent can add another dimension to interesting foliage. The scented-leaved pelargoniums, for example, come in many varieties with different fragrances, and are delightful in containers positioned where you can crush a leaf as you pass.

Cannas, tender perennials that are usually treated as annuals, have wonderful green or bronze leaves twirled around the stems as well as large brightly coloured flowers. The leaves are large and shiny, which, along with the hot flower colours, adds a touch of the exotic and tropical to any planting scheme.

WINTER

For winter schemes, ornamental cabbages (*Brassica oleracea*) are extremely valuable. The variegated leaves, in shades of pink or white, add a welcome touch of colour at a time when it may be in short supply.

Right: *The beautiful silver of the leaves and the wings on the stems of this* Onopordum acanthium, *or Scotch thistle, gives the plant a stunning appearance. This dramatic shape makes it one of the best architectural plants for beds and borders.*

POPULAR FOLIAGE ANNUALS

Abutilon megapotamicum 'Variegatum'
Ammobium alatum
Atriplex hortensis 'Rubra' (red orach)
Bassia (syn. *Kochia*) *scoparia trichophylla*
Beta vulgaris
Brassica oleracea (ornamental cabbage)
Canna
Coleus blumei (syn. *Solenostemon scutellarioides*)
Euphorbia marginata
Galactites tomentosa
Helichrysum petiolare
Impatiens (busy Lizzie – bronze-leaf forms)
Melianthus major (honeybush)
Ocimum basilicum 'Purple Ruffles'
Onopordum acanthium (Scotch thistle)
Pelargonium (geranium – scented-leaved forms)
Perilla frutescens
Ricinus communis (castor-oil plant)
Senecio cineraria (syn. *S. maritima*)
Silybum marianum
Tropaeolum majus 'Alaska'

Above: Helichrysum petiolare *is a tender perennial that is frequently used in both containers and bedding schemes, mainly for its furry, silvery-grey foliage.*

Above: *A favourite plant for self-sowing is the purple-leaved red orach (*Atriplex hortensis *'Rubra').
It looks best in a position in which the sun can shine through and light up the leaves.*

Right: *The red markings on this unusual and very striking annual,* Medicago echinus, *combine beautifully with the perennial* Geranium phaeum *'Samabor'.*

Annual Grasses

Annual grasses are not as popular as they deserve to be, possibly because in many people's minds annuals are synonymous with flowers, and grasses, perhaps, are associated with lawns. Ornamental grasses do have flowers but they are hardly brightly coloured things when compared with busy Lizzies (*Impatiens*) or pelargoniums. However, grasses have their own subtle charm, and are extremely useful for adding a quietening note to a scheme and for the swaying elegance they bring to mixed borders.

POPULAR ANNUAL GRASSES

Agrostis nebulosa
Briza maxima (greater quaking grass)
Briza minor (lesser quaking grass)
Hordeum jubatum (squirreltail grass)
Lagurus ovatus (hare's-tail grass)
Lamarckia aurea (golden top)
Panicum capillare (old-witch grass)
Pennisetum setaceum (African fountain grass)
Pennisetum villosum (feather top)
Sorghum nigrum
Zea mays (ornamental maize)

NATURAL GRACE

What grasses lack in colour they more than make up for in grace and beauty. They have elegant shapes; whether they are tall and wispy or stout clumps, grasses always exhibit the same kind of linear form. The leaves are long and straight. The flower stems are also long and narrow, and even in short grasses are usually taller than the leaves. Even the flowerheads tend to be long and narrow, but if they are spreading then the individual components are narrow, creating a wonderfully diffuse effect.

The numerous flower stems erupt like fountains, taking the eye with them and giving the display an upward thrust. At the same time their simplicity means that there is something cool about grasses. They move gracefully in the slightest breeze. They are gentle, even soothing to the eye, especially after the hurly-burly of conventional, colourful annuals.

USING GRASSES

Grasses can be used by themselves to create a distinct feature or they can be mixed in with other annuals. You are most likely to use them as a whole bedding scheme or as part of one, although they can also be grown in containers, particularly the taller ones. Generally, they are not much use in hanging baskets, but some of the arching types can be effective if used with care.

Most grasses are extremely good at catching the sunlight and can look superb when lit from behind. Place them so that they are between the viewer and the evening sun for some of the most stunning effects. Squirrel-tail grass (*Hordeum jubatum*), for example, creates a wonderful arching, feathery effect, and looks fantastic when it catches the sunlight.

Unfortunately, most of the annual grasses are quite short, although ornamental maize (*Zea mays*) will grow up to 2.4m (8ft) in a season, which is tall enough for most purposes. Most annual grasses have green leaves, but some have a distinct bronze tinge, while others, including ornamental maize, are variegated.

Many annual grasses can be dried and used as indoor decoration. Hare's-tail grass (*Lagurus ovatus*), which has chunky but very soft heads, is a popular drying grass. The feather top (*Pennisetum villosum*), strictly a perennial but a tender one, has more open heads, but again is wonderfully silky.

Below: *Soft grasses look very effective when they are backlit by sunlight, as this squirreltail grass (*Hordeum jubatum*) shows. Stirred by the breeze the effect is even more enchanting.*

Above: *Not all grasses associate well with flowering plants, but in this planting scheme squirreltail grass* (Hordeum jubatum*) makes a very effective partner for* Dahlia *'Yelno Harmony'.*

Above: *Arching grasses have a pleasing, often restful, effect. Here the tender perennial* Pennisetum setaceum *'Cupreum Compactum' adds a tranquil note, in contrast to more colourful plants.*

Above: *Many grasses are useful for drying as well as creating a decorative effect in the garden. The hare's-tail grass* (Lagurus ovatus*) is one such plant.*

Annuals in Pots and Planters

In the past annuals were mainly used as bedding plants in borders, but with the increased interest in container planting, including hanging baskets and window boxes, annuals have taken on a new lease of life, and they make the most perfect container plants.

USING ANNUALS

Containers are an immediate way of gardening, almost like flower arranging except that the flowers have roots. One minute the pot is empty, the next it is full of flowers. Annuals lend themselves to this style of gardening. They have such a short life cycle that they flower very early in their lives, soon after planting out, or they may already be in flower when planted.

Many have a long flowering period, often covering the whole of the summer and most of the autumn as well. They are also colourful, a factor that most people want in their containers. An added bonus is that they are relatively easy to look after: they just need watering and a bit of dead-heading.

Almost any annuals can be used in containers, though the very tall ones will usually be less successful. Scotch thistles (*Onopordum acanthium*), for example, would look out of proportion in a small pot, but could be effective in the centre of a large arrangement.

CONTAINERS

Containers can be used singly or in groups. An advantage of containers is that they can be moved around. Groups can be reformed or split up, constantly changing the scene. If one pot begins to look a bit straggly or the flowers fade, then it can be moved out of sight and perhaps another used to replace it. Collect as many different types and sizes of container as you can and use them imaginatively.

PLANTING TECHNIQUES

When planting a container, you will have to add crocks to the bottom in order to aid drainage. Plants in containers need plenty of water, but they do not like sitting in stagnant water, so it is important to ensure that any excess water can drain away easily. The compost (soil mix) can be either a general one or one that has been especially formulated for use in pots and other containers.

As care and attention are usually lavished on containers by way of daily watering and regular feeding, you can pack plants more tightly than you normally would in a bed or border. Keep the plants neat by removing dead heads and any straggly growths. The perfectionist always has a few spare plants tucked away out of sight to use as replacements if one of the plants in the container dies or begins to flag.

Left: *An evergreen cordyline has been livened up for the summer by the addition of colourful annuals. As the flowers die, different ones can replace them according to the seasons. For example, winter pansies are good plants to add interest to an evergreen shrub as they bloom non-stop right through the gloomier months and are not particularly affected by the weather.*

Below: *As this lovely container planting shows, there is nothing to beat the striking combination of pink and purple flowers with silver foliage.*

PLANTING CONTAINERS WITH ANNUALS

1 Before you start to plant, assemble all the materials you need: a container, crocks, perhaps a stone, compost (soil mix), water-retaining crystals, slow-release fertilizer, and your chosen plants and a trowel if you are using one. Pots can be heavy when they are filled with wet compost, so it is best to fill them where they are to be sited.

2 Ensure the container has drainage holes. Partially cover any large holes with an irregularly shaped stone, to prevent the compost (soil mix) falling out, then place other crocks in the bottom of the container to aid drainage.

3 Nearly fill the container with compost (soil mix) and add water-retaining crystals, following the manufacturer's instructions. Compost in containers dries out very quickly and these help reduce the amount of watering required. They swell up into a jelly-like substance, enabling the compost to retain much more water than it normally would.

4 Constant watering washes away many of the nutrients in the compost (soil mix) before the plants can take them up, so it is important to feed them regularly. Adding a slow-release fertilizer to the compost before planting provides food for several months, so you do not have to apply liquid feed regularly.

5 Fill the container with compost (soil mix) almost to the top and gently firm down. Make planting holes using a trowel or your hand and insert the plants to the same depth as they were in their pots or trays. Once all the plants are in position, firm and tidy up the compost, then water well.

6 Tidy up the container by cutting off any damaged stems. Tease out the stems to make the plants look natural and as if they have been planted for some time.

7 The finished container will look even more effective if grouped together with others. Remember to water containers regularly: even in winter, sun and wind can be quite drying, and in a hot summer they may need watering more than once a day.

Annuals in Window Boxes

By making use of wall space, window boxes allow for vertical gardening. This is particularly important where ground space is restricted, but it also helps to create a three-dimensional garden. Also, they are useful for transforming what otherwise may be a rather dull building or wall.

SAFETY

Window boxes are heavy when filled with moist soil, so if the site is windy and exposed, it is important that they are fixed securely. A falling window box is not only a broken and wasted window box, but it is extremely dangerous to anyone underneath. If you do not feel competent to fix it, ask a professional to do the job; it will be cheaper than any possible litigation resulting from a window box falling on someone's head.

MATERIALS

Window boxes are made of various different materials. Terracotta and replica stone look good but are heavy. Plastic ones usually look what they are, but they are lightweight and if covered with trailing plants cannot be seen. Wood is a compromise; it looks good and is reasonably lightweight, but it will eventually rot. Wood's big advantage is that the box can be tailor-made to fit the space.

PLANTS FOR WINDOW BOXES

The range of plants for window boxes is more limited than for pots. Choose a few upright, bushy plants for the rear and trailing ones for the front. For winter and spring use, it is often a good idea to use a few dwarf conifers or evergreen shrubs to give the box structure. You can also do this for summer, but with so many varieties of plants at your disposal it is not so necessary.

PLANTING TECHNIQUES

Place crocks in the bottom of the box to allow easy drainage. There are specially formulated composts (soil or planting mixes) for window boxes, but a general compost is usually more than adequate. Set the plants close together so that when they are in full growth no soil shows; a thinly planted window box can look rather sad and messy.

Keep the box well watered; every day is likely to be necessary. A special pump-action water dispenser with a long nozzle can be used to water them from the ground, but higher ones have to be watered from the window (site the box well below the window so that it will open) or from a ladder. Exercise caution if you use a ladder.

POSITIONING WINDOW BOXES

The obvious place for a window box is outside a window, but their shape and size means that they are suited to other positions. They are good for placing on the top of walls, for example, or on the ground, perhaps together with round pots.

Above: *Cheerful-looking pansies and lobelias are excellent plants for window boxes because they last for a long time and are very little trouble. Some varieties of pansy can also be used for winter displays. As this trough shows, long, box-like containers can be used successfully on the ground as well as on windowsills.*

PLANTING A WINDOW BOX WITH ANNUALS

1 Assemble all the ingredients: these include a window box, irregularly shaped stones, good quality compost (soil mix), water-retaining crystals, slow-release fertilizer, plants and a trowel if you are using one. If the box is light, assemble it on the ground. If it is heavy, make it up in position, especially if it is to be fixed high up.

2 Stagnant water can be a problem in inadequately drained boxes, so always buy, or make, boxes with holes in the bottom. Place irregularly shaped stones over the bottom of the box to help water drain down towards the holes. Partially cover the holes with these to stop compost (soil mix) falling through.

3 Partially fill the box with compost (soil mix), then mix in water-retaining crystals following the manufacturer's instructions. Continue to fill the box with compost, then gently firm down.

4 Make planting holes with a trowel or your hand and insert the plants to the same depths as they were in their pots or trays. Since you will be constantly watering and feeding the plants, it is possible to plant much more closely together than you would in open ground.

5 Since the window box will be watered frequently, the nutrients in the compost (soil mix) will quickly get washed away, so regular feeding is very important. This is traditionally done by adding a liquid feed to the water every week or so. Alternatively, slow-release fertilizer can be added, either in tablet form, as shown here, or as granules mixed into the compost (soil mix) before planting. Both of these should supply sufficient food for the season.

6 Water the window box thoroughly. The box still looks under-filled, but the plants will soon grow and spread out to fill the whole box. If it is possible to plant a box away from its final position, it can be filled with plants and left for a while until they are all in full flower before being displayed.

7 Boxes that are heavier than this one should be filled in position so that they do not have to be carried and lifted. As well as avoiding physical damage to the gardener, it also prevents the plants being damaged in transit.

Annuals in Hanging Baskets

Hanging baskets are ever increasing in popularity and seed merchants and plant suppliers are constantly searching out new annuals to feed demand. There are now so many bushy and trailing plants to choose from, you can really let your imagination run riot. There is even a trailing variety of tomato, 'Tumbler', which not only looks attractive but provides the added bonus of a crop of delicious fruit.

THE BASKETS

Baskets consist of three parts: the basket, a liner and a support, frequently a chain. The baskets are usually made from plastic-coated wire. Increasingly they are also available in just plastic but these do not look as good (if you can see them under the plants) and can become brittle.

Liners can be made of compressed paper, coir (coconut fibre) matting or moss. Moss is the most natural-looking but stocks in the wild are being threatened by over-collecting. Paper is recycled and coir is cultivated, so both of these are environmentally acceptable.

You can use either a good general-purpose compost (soil mix) or a specially formulated hanging-basket compost which includes water-retaining gel or crystals. In this case, do not add further gel or crystals, as excessive quantities would cause problems when they expand.

PLANTING HANGING BASKETS

Most hanging baskets include tender annuals so they cannot be placed outside until after the last frosts, but they can be made up in advance and left indoors until the danger of frosts has passed, by which time the basket will have filled out and with luck be in full flower.

Plant the hanging basket tightly so that there are few spaces between the plants. This is acceptable as there should be no shortage of moisture and nutrients if the basket is regularly watered and fed. As well as planting the surface of the compost (soil mix), it is also possible to make holes through the liner so that plants can be inserted around the sides. The most successful baskets are those in which the framework cannot be seen, as it is entirely masked by plants. In many cases, the hanging basket will look like a ball of plants.

A wide range of plants are available for baskets and an increasing number of trailing ones are being introduced. Many plants, such as pelargoniums and petunias, have trailing varieties as well as the more common bushy ones. Even snapdragons have been bred with a trailing habit. Any combination of plants can be used to create different schemes. A wonderful pot-pourri of colours can be achieved with a mixed planting, although a much more sophisticated effect can be created if you use plants in the same colour or even plants of just one variety. Baskets can be used individually or grouped together to produce a grander effect.

Above: *Hanging baskets like this can be very heavy so make sure that the fixing point is strong enough. Check each year that it is still secure before replanting the hanging basket.*

POPULAR ANNUALS FOR HANGING BASKETS

Anagallis	*Laurentia* (syn. *Isotoma*)
Antirrhinum (snapdragon)	*Lobelia*
Asarina	*Myosotis* (forget-me-not)
Begonia	*Nicotiana* (tobacco plant)
Bidens	*Pelargonium* (geranium)
Brachycome	*Petunia*
Camissonia	*Sanvitalia*
Cerinthe	*Schizanthus* (butterfly flower, poor man's orchid)
Chrysanthemum	
Diascia	*Senecio*
Echium	*Tagetes* (marigold)
Felicia	*Tropaeolum* (nasturtium)
Fuchsia	
Helichrysum	*Viola* × *wittrockiana* (pansy)

PLANTING A HANGING BASKET WITH ANNUALS

1 Assemble all the ingredients for making up the hanging basket, including compost (soil mix), water-retaining crystals and slow-release fertilizer.

2 Stand the basket on a large pot or bucket to make it easier to work with. Carefully place the liner in position so that it fills the basket.

3 Half fill the liner with compost (soil mix), then mix in some water-retaining crystals following the manufacturer's instructions to help prevent the basket drying out. Also add some slow-release fertilizer; this will remove the necessity to feed throughout the summer.

4 Cut holes about 4cm (1½in) across in the side of the liner. Shake some of the earth off the rootball of one of the side plants and wrap it in a strip of plastic. Poke it through the hole, remove the plastic and spread the roots out. When all the side plants are in place, fill up the basket with compost (soil mix), adding more water-retaining crystals and slow-release fertilizer.

5 Plant up the rest of the basket, packing the plants much more tightly together than you would in the open ground. Smooth out the surface of the compost (soil mix), removing any excess or adding a little more as necessary. Water, then hang the basket indoors until all danger of frost has passed.

Above: *The various types of pelargoniums are well suited to planting in a hanging basket. They make very cheerful planting partners. Here they are contrasted with verbena and trailing lobelia.*

PROPAGATION AND PLANTING

Sowing Seed in Rows

There are several ways to sow annuals. Hardy annuals can be sown directly in the soil, in either spring or autumn. For speed, most half-hardy or tender annuals are sown under glass but many can also be sown directly in the open soil once the threat of frosts is past.

BIENNIALS

Biennials such as wallflowers (*Erysimum*) or sweet Williams (*Dianthus barbatus*) are the type of plant that are most frequently sown outside in rows, in a spare piece of ground, rather than in the positions where they are intended to flower. Since they take a year to come into flower, it is not usually desirable for them to take up valuable bedding or border space during their growing stage when, visually, not much is happening. It is therefore a good idea to find some space for them in the vegetable garden or in specially allocated nursery beds. They are sown in the spring then planted in their flowering positions in the autumn, after the current year's annuals have finished flowering and been cleared away.

SOWING

Before you begin sowing, you need to prepare the ground thoroughly. Remove all the perennial weeds, preferably during the autumn before sowing so that the soil can lie fallow during the winter.

In the spring break the soil down into a fine tilth. Using a garden line and a hoe draw out a shallow drill in the soil. If there has not been much rain, the soil will be dry. So, water along the drill (alternatively, you can water after the drill has been raked over) and then sow the seed thinly. Rake the soil back over the seed. Mark the row with two sticks, one at each end, and a label. This is important as you will surprised how quickly you forget what you have planted and this will make it difficult to plan planting schemes when you eventually transplant the seedlings.

When the seedlings have germinated, thin out the plants to 10–15cm (4–6in) apart. Keep them weed-free and water during dry spells. In the autumn move the plants to their flowering positions, having first rejuvenated the soil by removing weeds and digging it over, adding plenty of well-rotted organic material.

As well as biennials, annuals for cutting and spare plants to use as replacements in bedding schemes or containers can be grown in this way. The advantage of sowing hardy annuals in the autumn is that they are already in flower at the time the spring-sown ones are being planted out. Combined with the spring-sown plants they create a longer flowering season.

Above: Dianthus barbatus *'Messenger Mixed', a biennial, can be sown outside in open ground and takes a year to come into flower.*

Above: *Pot marigolds (*Calendula officinalis*) come into flower much earlier if they are sown in the open ground during the autumn.*

SOWING IN ROWS

1 Prepare the ground thoroughly, digging it over and breaking it down into a fine tilth using a rake. Do not work the soil when it is too wet or it will become compacted.

2 Using a garden line as a guide, draw out a shallow drill. Use the corner of a hoe, a stick or a trowel.

ANNUALS FOR AUTUMN SOWING

Agrostemma githago (corn cockle)
Calendula officinalis (pot marigold)
Centaurea cyanus (cornflower)
Collinsia grandiflora
Consolida ambigua, syn. *C. ajacis* (larkspur)
Eschscholzia californica
Gypsophila elegans
Iberis umbellata
Lathyrus odoratus (sweet pea)
Limnanthes douglasii (poached-egg plant)
Myosotis (forget-me-not)
Nigella damascena (love-in-a-mist)
Papaver rhoeas (field poppy)
Scabiosa atropurpurea (sweet scabious)

3 If the soil is very dry, water the drill using a watering can and leave to drain. It should not be muddy for sowing.

4 Identify the row with a clearly labelled marker. This is especially important because when the row is backfilled it will be impossible to see where the seed is until it germinates.

5 Sow the seed along the drill. Sow thinly to reduce the amount of thinning required.

6 Rake the soil back over the drill and lightly tamp it down with the back of the rake. When the seedlings emerge, thin them out to prevent overcrowding.

Sowing Seed in Situ

Most annuals that are sown directly in the open soil are sown in situ, that is they are sown where they are to flower. This method is usually used for plants that are going to flower in drifts or blocks rather than intricate patterns. It can be used for autumn-sown plants but it is more usually used for seed sown after the frosts have passed in late spring. By then the soil has warmed up and usually annuals germinate very quickly and soon reach flowering size.

PREPARING THE GROUND

Prepare the ground well, preferably in autumn, removing all weeds and breaking it down to a fine tilth. In some cases the planting will be among perennials or some other permanent planting and so the area will already be defined, but if it is a large bed, broken up into several different blocks or areas, then some pre-planning will be required.

Work out on paper the shapes and locations of the various blocks or drifts of plants. The design can be precise or rough, depending on the accuracy you want to achieve. Transfer this outline to the ground by trailing sand, from either your hand or a bottle, around each area. For precise marking first draw a grid over the design on paper then create an equivalent grid on the bed using canes and string. Using the grids as guides transfer the design exactly on to the ground.

SOWING

Once the area has been marked out to your satisfaction, the seed can be sown. There are two methods. The first is to broadcast the seed over the allocated space, simply by taking a handful of seed and scattering it evenly over the soil. The second is to draw out short parallel rows, not too far apart, across the area and sow into these. The first is quicker and creates a natural looking effect, but broadcasting evenly can be difficult and there may be bald areas. The second takes more time but ensures a more even coverage, and also makes weeding easier as you can hoe between rows. Although sown in rows, a random look can be achieved by careful thinning.

If you want the various blocks to merge, scatter a little of the seed into the next area so that the line between adjacent plantings becomes blurred once the plants have matured.

THINNING

Unless you have sown the seed very thinly, you will need to thin out the plants once they have germinated. If you are planning a formal bedding scheme then thin out at regular distances, to create a pattern. Alternatively, for a more natural look, thin at random intervals. If the seed was sown in rows, removing plants at irregular intervals will help break up the lines. Replant a few if necessary to create a still more random effect.

1 Thoroughly prepare the ground by digging the soil and breaking it down into a fine tilth using a rake. Do not work the soil when it is too wet or it will become compacted.

2 If you are planning to use several different blocks of plants, mark out the design on the soil using contrasting coloured sand or compost (soil mix).

3 Broadcast the seed by hand so that it is thinly spread right across the appropriate area. It will probably be necessary to thin out the seedlings when they appear.

4 Gently rake the seed in so that it is covered by a thin layer of soil.

5 Some gardeners prefer to sow in short rows rather than broadcasting. This makes it easier to weed when the seed first comes up. Draw out shallow drills with a hoe.

6 Sow the seed thinly along each row and rake the soil back over them. By carefully thinning the seedlings the resulting overall pattern of the plants will appear to be random and not in rows.

7 Finally, gently water the whole bed, using a watering can fitted with a fine rose.

8 A bed planted with annuals begins to fill out soon after sowing and planting.

Above: *This delightful annual relative of the delphinium,* Consolida ambigua, *can be sown directly into the open border.*

Sowing Seed in Pots

Most annuals are grown from seed sown in trays or pots. The conditions under which they germinate are much more under the gardener's control than those outside. A late frost, for example, should not affect them as they can be kept under cover. However, growing annuals this way does mean a lot more work than sowing outside.

POTS OR TRAYS?

Seed can be sown in either trays or pots. When they first start to garden, many people sow all their seed in trays, but this can be a waste of expensive compost (soil mix) and time as well as taking up valuable propagator and greenhouse space. Seed sown in a 9cm (3½in) pot will produce enough seedlings for most gardening purposes. For larger quantities, if you are planning a large bedding scheme for example, where a lot of plants are required, then sow in a half or full tray. The basic method for dealing with seedlings is the same for both pots and trays.

SOWING

Fill the pot with compost (soil mix) and lightly press it down. Scatter the seed thinly over the surface of the compost. Do not be tempted to sow the whole packet if you only want a few plants. A few seedlings spread evenly over the surface of a pot or tray get a better start in life than overcrowded ones. The latter quickly become overdrawn and starved, and never properly recover from such treatment.

The traditional method of covering seed is to sieve a thin layer of compost over it, but many gardeners prefer to cover it with a layer of grit about 5–10mm (¼–½in) deep. The thickness of the covering should be roughly equivalent to the size of the seed. Water the seed with a watering can fitted with a fine rose and place in a propagator which is set to the temperature recommended on the seed packet. If you are not in a hurry, most seed will eventually germinate if left in an unheated greenhouse as long as the temperature is not allowed to fall below freezing.

As an alternative to the above method, it is also possible to sow the seed singly or in twos and threes in modules or cells. Once the seeds have germinated, pull out any excess plants leaving one per cell. The advantage of this is that the seedlings do not need to be pricked out and potted on, thus avoiding the growth of the plants being checked.

Plants in a propagator do not need to be covered as the unit provides an enclosed atmosphere. However, if a pot of seed is put on an open bench or indoors, then it should be covered with a sheet of glass or a piece of cling film (plastic wrap) or enclosed in a plastic bag. Once the seeds have germinated, uncover the pot to allow air to circulate. A propagator is usually large enough to leave the plants enclosed.

SOWING SEED

1 There is a wide range of equipment that can be used for sowing seed, but there is no necessity to use anything other than basic items such as small pots, seed trays or a simple propagator.

2 Using a good seed compost (soil mix), fill either a pot or a tray and gently firm it down, using the base of another pot or tray, so that the surface is level and just below that of the container.

3 Thinly scatter the seeds across the surface of the compost (soil mix). Thickly sown seed means that the resulting seedlings are drawn and starved, which may result in poor quality plants.

4 Cover the seeds with a thin layer of grit, fine gravel or compost. Grit prevents the surface compacting and will make for more even watering. It also keeps the necks of the seedlings dry, helping to prevent them rotting.

5 Water the pot of seed with a watering can fitted with a fine rose. Alternatively, stand the pot in a tray of water until the grit changes colour, indicating that the compost (soil mix) is thoroughly wetted.

6 Label the container, then place it in a propagator. This can be unheated, as here, or heated to the recommended temperature for that seed, which will produce quicker germination.

7 Ensure that the compost (soil mix) in the pots stays moist and that the temperature does not drop below about 15 degrees C (60 degrees F), and the seed will soon germinate.

8 Seed can also be sown in cellular trays. This avoids the need for pricking out, saving time and reducing root disturbance. Place two or three seeds in each cell, and remove all but the best seedling when they have germinated.

Pricking Out and Hardening Off

Once the seed has germinated, it is important to prick out the seedlings before they become too large and overcrowded. Pricking out is simply planting each seedling in its own patch of compost (soil mix). This may be in its own pot or it may be with others in a tray but planted in such a way that it has space to develop.

PREPARING THE SEEDLINGS

If your pot or tray of seedlings has started life in an enclosed propagator the seedlings will need to be hardened off or acclimatized to the greenhouse's atmosphere, otherwise they may not recover from the shock of being moved to a cooler, drier atmosphere. Wean them out of the propagator over a couple of days by allowing more air into the propagator, eventually taking off the lid completely. Do not do this if the temperature in the greenhouse can drop below freezing; if it can, the seedlings need to be returned to the warm propagator after potting up. If the seedlings have been grown on the open bench there is no problem with acclimatization.

PRICKING OUT

As with sowing seed, you can use pots or trays for pricking out. If the plants will not have to remain in them too long, trays are ideal for producing mass bedding plants, but if they are to be left some time before planting out, or you want reasonably sized plants, it will be better to prick out into individual pots. Larger specimen plants such as pelargoniums are better off in pots where there is more root space and less competition.

Loosely fill the pot with a good potting compost (soil mix). Gently firm it down and make a hole in the centre with your finger or a dibber. Gently tip the contents of the pot or tray on to the bench. Remove the seedlings one at a time, holding them by a leaf, not by the stem or roots, as they will recover more easily from a damaged leaf. Lower a plant into the hole and gently fill around it with more compost. For larger plants, hold the plant over the centre of the empty pot and pour compost around it. Firm down gently.

Trays should be similarly filled with compost and a series of holes made before lowering a plant into each one.

Gently water and place on a greenhouse bench, out of direct sunlight and draughts (drafts), or in a cold frame. Do not allow the young plants to dry out.

HARDENING OFF

A couple of weeks before you need to plant out, start to harden the plants off. If you have a cold frame, gradually open the frame a little further each day until it is fully open. From a greenhouse, place the plants in the open for a few hours each day, gradually increasing the time until they are permanently in the open air.

1 If the seedlings have been in a heated propagator, harden them off to the greenhouse temperature before pricking out, by gradually opening the propagator vents over a couple of days. Gently knock out the pot of seedlings on to the bench.

2 Gently break open the ball of soil so that it is easier to remove the seedlings one by one.

3 Separate the seedlings one at a time as each is required. Always lift and carry a seedling by its leaves, never its roots or stem. Use a label or dibber to ease the seedling from the compost (soil mix) without tearing the roots.

4 Hold the seedling over the centre of the pot, keeping your hand steady against the side of the pot, and pour good quality potting compost (soil mix) around it until the pot is full to the brim.

5 Tap the pot on the bench to settle the compost (soil mix) and then gently firm down with your thumbs or fingers so that the final level is below the rim of the pot.

6 A similar process is carried out with trays. Fill with compost (soil mix) to the brim and then gently firm down.

7 Prick out the seedlings into the tray, making a hole for each seedling with your finger or a dibber. Fill in with compost (soil mix) and gently firm down. Space the seedlings out evenly across the tray.

8 Water the pots or trays with a watering can fitted with a fine rose. Keep the seedlings in the greenhouse or somewhere warm until they have started growing away, then harden them off over a week or more by allowing them increasing amounts of time in the open air, or with a cold frame, by gradually opening it.

Buying Seedlings and Plants

Not everybody is able or wants to grow their own plants. This may be because they have not got the facilities or the time, or simply because growing everything from seed does not appeal to them. The easy option is to buy young plants from a garden centre or nursery.

ADVANTAGES AND DISADVANTAGES

There are advantages and disadvantages to buying plants. The advantages include convenience because the plants are usually ready to plant out. If you had planned to sow seeds but left it too late, you can simply buy the plants and get back on schedule.

The main disadvantage is that your choice may be restricted. There is always a much wider choice of seed in a seed merchant's catalogue than there are plants in a nursery or at a local garden centre. Very often you will find that colour choice is restricted. For example, snapdragons (*Antirrhinum*) may be offered as seed in a whole range of single colours as well as tall or short plants, or even different types of flower. If you buy annuals such as these as plants, you may be offered only trays of mixed colours with no other options.

Another disadvantage is that the plants may have been grown too closely together or left in their packs for far too long. Either way they will be drawn and not particularly healthy looking specimens. Finally, as long as you do not take the demands on your time into account, growing from seed is also much cheaper, and more rewarding.

QUALITY

When buying annuals – or any plant for that matter – always check you are happy with the quality. Reject plants that are drawn, tall and spindly as a result of lack of light and competition from the other plants in the pack. Avoid them if they are potbound, in other words if the pot or tray is a solid mass of roots. Annuals that are potbound very rarely send their roots out into the surrounding soil and will always remain half-starved.

It is important never to buy plants that look sickly, are obviously diseased in any way or are covered with insect pests. You will be making difficulties for yourself, because not only will these plants never develop into anything, they may well also transmit pests and diseases to existing healthy plants growing in your garden.

Plants are sold in a range of containers. Individual pots are the best as plants have room to develop in them, but they are liable to be the most expensive. Cells or strips will be much cheaper and as long as the plants are not too old or crowded should prove satisfactory. Plants can be purchased by mail order when they are liable to come as 'plugs', that is individual plantlets either bare-rooted or in cells. Pot these up and grow them on for a bit before planting out.

A SELECTION OF CONTAINERS

1 Grown individually in packs, young plants have plenty of room to develop a good root system. Plants can stay in these larger packs longer and with less fear of being overcrowded.

2 In packs of plugs, young plants are grown in small cells. These are cheaper than those in larger packs, but make sure they have not become potbound, starved and drawn through being left too long in the cells where the tangled mass of roots will not be able to find enough food. The plants should be potted on and allowed to grow for a while before planting out.

3 Some of the best plants come in individual pots, but they are much more expensive to buy as more work and attention were required to raise them. The plants have more compost (soil mix) in which to grow and can be left in them longer than when in packs or plugs.

4 When choosing plants always check the root system. It should be evenly spread and not overcrowded (right). If the roots have wound themselves around the inside of the pot and are obviously overcrowded (left), then reject the plant.

Above: *In this lovely hanging basket, the plants have not only trailed over the edge but climbed up the chain, creating the effect of a waterfall of plants. Such strong-growing individuals were probably purchased in pots.*

Taking Cuttings of Tender Perennials

Tender perennials, in their native warm climate, would survive from year to year, and you can keep them over the winter by removing them from the garden and taking them indoors, into a heated greenhouse, for example, or even a spare bedroom. There seems little point in throwing them away every year only to replace them with new ones. Some grow too old and overgrown and rather than replant them the following year it makes more sense to take cuttings from them and start them afresh. This is also a good way to increase the number of plants. If you buy one pelargonium one year, by the next you can have a dozen or more identical plants.

TAKING CUTTINGS

Taking cuttings of tender perennials such as pelargoniums is much easier than many people imagine. You can take cuttings as soon as you remove the plants in late autumn and overwinter them, so they will be rooted and ready to plant out in spring. Or you can leave the plants in their pots in the warm and take the cuttings in the spring. The advantage of the first option is that the plants will be much bigger by planting out time. Also, overwintering a plant as cuttings minimizes the chances of losing that plant as it is unlikely that all the cuttings would die.

On the other hand, leaving the task until the spring has the advantage that you only have one plant to look after over the winter, which may be a consideration if your space is limited. Also, gardeners can often feel as jaded and tired as their gardens in the autumn and may simply not feel like bothering with cuttings at this time of year.

Cuttings should be taken from healthy stems. If there is any chance that you may not be dealing with them straight away, put them into a plastic bag to prevent them wilting. Cut just below a node (the point where the leaf joins the stem). Trim off all the leaves above except for the last pair. Most annuals root easily without recourse to a rooting powder or liquid, but some growers like to use them as they contain fungicide that helps to prevent disease entering the cuts. If you do decide to use them, dip the rooting end into the powder or liquid before inserting it into a cutting compost (soil mix).

Place the cuttings around the edge of a 9cm (3½in) pot filled with a cutting compost (soil mix) or a mixture of 50 per cent sharp sand and 50 per cent peat (or peat substitute). Place this in a propagator or substitute propagator such as a plastic bag, supported above the plants with sticks if necessary, or the bottom of a plastic bottle.

It is usually obvious when roots have formed as the cutting begins to grow away and roots appear through the holes in the bottom of the pot. Separate the cuttings and pot them up individually.

HOW TO TAKE CUTTINGS

1 You only need a few basic tools and materials: expensive propagators are unnecessary. A sharp knife, small scissors, pots, a pencil or dibber, markers and a simple propagator or plastic bottles are all you require. Buy or make up a cutting compost (soil mix): a 50:50 mixture of sharp sand and peat or peat substitute is ideal.

2 Fill a 9cm (3½in) pot with compost (soil mix), tap it on the bench and gently firm it down.

3 Take cuttings only from healthy, pest-free plants. Water the plant a few hours before taking the cuttings. Remove a shoot and cut it into 7.5cm (3in) lengths, cutting just beneath a leaf joint. Avoid using stems that have or have had flowers on them.

4 Trim off side shoots and any leaves on the stem except for the top pair. Make the cuts cleanly using a sharp knife or scissors. Do not leave any snags (pieces of side shoots or leaf stems) on the cutting.

5 Using a pencil or dibber, insert the cuttings around the edge of the pot, so that they do not touch one another. A 9cm (3½in) pot will accommodate 6–12 cuttings, depending on their size.

6 Water the cuttings using a watering can fitted with a fine rose. Indoors, a better way of watering is to stand the pot in a tray of water until the surface of the compost (soil mix) changes colour as it becomes damp.

7 Place the pot in a close atmosphere. A propagator is best if you have one, but the bottom of a plastic bottle or even a plastic bag makes a very good substitute. Place in a warm, but not sunny, position.

8 When the cuttings show roots through the bottom of the pot, pot them up into individual pots using a good quality potting compost (soil mix). They will then grow away and develop into healthy plants.

Preparing the Ground

To give your plants the best chance of success, you need to ensure that the soil is in good condition. Preparing the ground thoroughly before you begin planting may seem like a lot of work, but the results will make it worthwhile.

WEEDS

The first task before planting out your seedlings is to get rid of any weeds. If the beds have been in use for several seasons, then they are probably already free of perennial weeds and the few annual weeds can be easily removed by hand or hoeing. However, if it is a new bed or ground that has become infested with perennial weeds, it must be cleaned thoroughly.

In light or crumbly ground many of the weeds can be extracted by hand. If it is heavy and mainly clay, however, you may have to resort to a herbicide. Most gardeners are not keen on using chemicals, but if you use them once only, making a thorough job of it and following the manufacturer's instructions, there is little chance of harm or a chemical build-up in your soil. Avoid making a half-hearted attempt and thus having to continue pumping in chemicals until you come to rely on them.

DIGGING

Dig the ground in the autumn if possible and let it lie fallow during the winter. By spring any remaining weeds should show up and can be easily removed. The weather will also have broken down the soil. When digging, incorporate as much well-rotted organic material as you can. Garden compost, farmyard manure, leafmould or proprietary brands of soil conditioner can all be used. As well as adding nutrients, these will help break down heavy soil, improving drainage, while enhancing moisture retention in light, free-draining soil.

In the spring, when the soil has lost some of its winter wetness and you can work on it without compacting it, break it down with a rake to a fine tilth. It is then ready for planting.

MARKING OUT BEDS

The outside of straight-sided beds can be marked with a garden line or canes. For curved and irregular beds a hosepipe (garden hose), rope or length of loose string can be used. When the shape looks satisfactory go round it with a spade or hoe, marking the outline on the ground. If the bed is in an existing lawn, the mower can be taken round the shape to mark its edge ready to start digging.

SOIL CONDITIONERS

Chipped or composted bark *Reasonable*
Farmyard manure *Good*
Garden compost *Excellent*
Leafmould *Excellent*
Peat *Poor*
Seaweed *Excellent*
Spent hops *Good*
Spent mushroom compost *Good*

MAKING A NEW BED

1 Mark out the bed with a garden line or, as here, with canes. It is important to remove all perennial weeds. This can be done with a weedkiller, which should be applied according to the maker's instructions on the packet. Leave the bed until all the weeds have died.

2 Alternatively the weeds can be removed by hand. This can be achieved by hoeing off the weeds or turf and then removing the remaining roots as you dig. If time allows, weeds can be killed off by covering the intended bed with black polythene for a couple of months before digging.

3 Start digging the bed by making a trench one spit (spade's depth) deep across one end. Place the excavated soil into a wheelbarrow and take it to the other end of the plot where it will be used to fill in the final trench.

4 Place a layer of well-rotted organic material such as garden compost or farmyard manure along the bottom of the trench.

5 Dig the next row, tipping the soil on top of the compost, filling in the first trench and creating a new one. Add compost to the bottom of this and repeat until the whole plot is dug leaving the final trench empty.

6 Add a layer of compost to the final trench and then fill it in using the soil excavated from the first trench. The digging is now complete and if time allows, you can leave the bed over the winter so the weather will break the soil down.

7 If prepared in the autumn, by the spring the weather will have broken down the soil to a fine tilth. Remove any weeds that have reappeared and then rake over the bed, using the back of the rake to break up any larger lumps if necessary.

Planting Out

There is always something rather satisfying about planting out plants; of all the garden jobs it seems the most fundamental. You see a patch of bare earth transformed into one full of promise of the colourful season ahead.

PREPARATION

Before planting it is essential to prepare the ground thoroughly (largely by removing any weeds) as described on the previous pages. Without such preparation the promise will never be fulfilled, or at best only in a half-hearted way. Another thing to do before planting, this time only a couple of hours before starting, is to ensure that all the containers of plants are thoroughly watered. This will give the plants time to absorb plenty of moisture so that they will not languish when first planted. Another advantage of doing this some time in advance is that the compost (soil mix) will have a chance to dry out somewhat. Handling sodden rootballs is neither desirable nor pleasant.

If the plants are in individual pots, place them where they are to be planted so that you get some idea of their distribution and whether it looks the way you want. This is not such a good idea if they are in strips, as the roots will dry out if left lying on the bare soil.

PLANTING

For each plant dig a hole wider than the rootball. Adjust the bottom of the hole so that the plant is set at the same depth as it was in the tray or pot. Put the plant in, push the soil in around it and firm in.

Once in position, water and then rake the surface of the soil around the plants in order to neaten it up. It is a good idea to mulch around the plants with a layer of well-rotted organic material. This will help to conserve moisture and keep the weeds down. In many cases, once the annuals have become fully developed they will form their own mulch.

Below: *This is a good example of a mixed border filled with plenty of annuals that were planted out in the early summer after the threat of frosts had passed.*

PLANTING SEEDLINGS

1 Several hours before planting, or the evening before, water the tray of annuals so that they are growing well and less likely to be stressed by the move.

2 Remove a plant from the pack by pressing on the bottom so that it slides out. In strips, where the plants are not segregated, remove the lot from the pack and carefully pull one from the group, trying not to tear off too many of its neighbour's roots.

3 Dig a hole wider and slightly deeper than the rootball.

4 Adjust the depth of the hole so that the top of the rootball is level with the surrounding soil.

5 Fill in the hole around the plant with soil and gently firm down with your hands.

6 Water the plant with a watering can fitted with a fine rose.

MAINTENANCE

Watering and Feeding

To a certain extent annuals in the open ground will look after themselves, but like all plants they will do better if they are given a bit of attention. Plants tightly packed in containers and hanging baskets, however, will need quite a lot of attention, although this is mainly restricted to watering and feeding.

Containers may even need watering after it has rained, the rain being shed beyond the rim of the pot by the foliage. During the winter, plants usually take up less moisture and rain is more prevalent, so less watering is necessary.

The constant passage of water through a container quickly leaches out any nutrients in the compost (soil mix). However, modern container composts include a slow-release fertilizer which should last the whole season. These can also be added to ordinary composts when the container is filled. An alternative is to add a liquid feed to every third or fourth watering.

OPEN GROUND

In the open ground plants find most of the moisture and nutrients that they need to grow. Many annuals originate in the hotter, drier regions of the world and do not need a great deal of water in order to survive. However, they may still need watering during prolonged dry spells, and some, such as sweet peas, do need plenty of moisture.

It is important to watch out for signs of flagging, usually indicated by the leaves beginning to droop. Water straight away if you see these signs. There are several means of watering. Watering cans or sprinklers are the most common. In either case make certain that the plants receive a thorough soaking. Just wetting the surface of the soil encourages the plants to produce shallow roots, making them less able to find moisture deep down.

In general, there is no need to feed plants in the open ground, but on poor soil or in a wet season, when the nutrients are leached from the soil by rain, it may be helpful to apply a liquid feed every two to three weeks.

CONTAINERS

Containers, including window boxes and baskets, need daily attention. They dry out quickly and tightly packed plants use up large quantities of water. In very hot or drying weather, they need watering twice or even three times a day. Watering can be reduced a little by adding water-retaining granules to the compost (soil mix) at the time of planting. These absorb up to three times their own volume of water and slowly release it to the roots. This helps, but you still need to water every day in hot weather.

Watering may be carried out using a watering can or a hand-held spray attached to a hosepipe (garden hose). As with plants in the open, water well. Remember that if a pot dries out it is difficult to re-wet the compost; the water tends to run between the compost and the side of the container. Give it a good soaking so that the water penetrates right to the centre. Baskets can be watered from the ground using a pump-action watering device with a long hooked nozzle that can reach above the operator's head.

WATERING AND FEEDING METHODS

1 One of the easiest ways of watering is with a watering can. This allows you to deliver just the right amount of water to each plant. However, it is only really suitable for containers or a small number of plants. Always make certain that the soil is well soaked, and that you have not just dampened the surface.

2 A rose fitted to a can (top) produces a gentle application of water, but for more direct watering aimed at the base of a particular plant, water through the spout can be a better option.

3 A sprinkler is the most efficient method of watering larger beds or borders. However, it is no use putting it on for a few minutes, it needs to give the ground a good soaking. Place a rain gauge or even a jar within the area sprayed to measure the amount of water delivered.

4 For larger quantities of containers or for hand-watering a border a spray attached to a hose is a better method. If the spray is on a lance then your reach is all the greater and it is easier to apply water to individual plants.

5 Much water is lost from the ground by evaporation. Covering the soil with a mulch helps to reduce this loss and make more available to the plants. An organic-based mulch such as chipped or composted bark is attractive and efficient. Place it right up to the stems of the plants.

6 Applying fertilizer in a liquid form is easy, simply add the required amount to a watering can when carrying out routine watering. With containers and other frequently watered areas feed once a week; in the open ground it can be less frequent.

7 For borders a special attachment can be purchased which delivers a prescribed amount of fertilizer when you water with a hose. The spray usually comes pre-loaded with fertilizer but refills can be purchased.

8 Solid fertilizers can be scattered on the ground around the plant, being careful not to get any on the leaves. Apply the fertilizer at the manufacturer's recommended dosage, as given on the package.

Pinching Out, Dead-heading and Trimming

Annuals generally have a long flowering season, often extending from early summer into the autumn and sometimes beyond. Needless to say, they will need a little bit of attention from time to time in order to keep them looking neat.

PINCHING OUT

If left to their own devices, many plants will grow only one main stem. In a bedding scheme, for example, this would result in a forest of tall spindly spikes with large gaps in between them rather than a desirable carpet of flowers and foliage. To avoid this effect, pinch out the growing tip of each main spike. This will cause the stem to produce side shoots. These will make the plants much more bushy, and further pinching out will increase the effect.

DEAD-HEADING

As the season progresses, flowers appear, then die, once they have been pollinated and have served their purpose. The petals go brown and look ugly, spoiling the effect of the still perfect flowers around them. Regular dead-heading keeps everything neat and tidy and looking in much better condition.

Another good reason for regular dead-heading is to prevent seed formation. Producing seed is the natural goal of every annual, and once they have been pollinated, they direct all their energy into forming the seeds, then die. If their fading flowers are removed,

they will redirect their energy into producing more flowers and so prolong their usefulness to the gardener.

TRIMMING BACK

New flowers are normally produced towards the tips of shoots, so as the season progresses and more and more flowers are produced, the stems get longer and longer. Before too long the plants begin to look somewhat straggly. Cut these stems back every so often so that new shoots are formed, keeping the plant compact. You can do this all at once but the plant may take a while to recover its flowering habit, so it is preferable to cut a few off at a time to prevent any interruption in flowering.

TOOLS

Secateurs (pruners) are the most versatile of tools, especially those that have pointed jaws so that you can get right into the leaf joints. Strong pointed scissors are also useful, especially for small plants. Knives can be used in most situations as long as they are sharp. Many stems can be snapped or pinched out with the fingers or fingernails, but make certain that the action is clean-cut and does not bruise the stem.

PINCHING OUT

1 Many annuals will grow up as a single stem, making rather spindly growth. However, if the tip is pinched out, side shoots will develop and the plant will become bushy and much more attractive. Cut through the stem with secateurs or a knife, just above a leaf joint.

2 The pinched-out plants fill out, creating a solid mass of attractive foliage. Planted together they make an attractive mass planting.

DEAD-HEADING

1 Dead heads left on plants, especially light-coloured flowers as seen here, look very scruffy if they are not removed regularly. Another good reason for dead-heading is to redirect the energy that would normally go into seed production into producing new flowers.

2 Using scissors, a sharp knife or secateurs, snip off the flowers neatly and cleanly where they join the stem. Sometimes the whole head of flowers needs to be removed, in which case cut these back to the first set of leaves. Dead flower heads and other clippings can be added to the compost heap.

TIDYING UP

3 Regular and carefully executed dead-heading produces a much cleaner and healthier looking arrangement. It takes only a short time and the effort is worthwhile.

1 Some edging plants spread out over the grass, possibly killing it or creating bald patches, as has this poached egg plant (*Limnanthes douglasii*).

2 If the plant has finished flowering, as here, it can be removed completely. Otherwise, just cut back the part that is encroaching on grass. On a brick or stone path, there may be no problem, though it could still cause people to stumble.

Staking and Protecting

Generally, most annuals manage quite well without any extra supports or protection, but occasionally, especially in exposed areas, it is necessary to provide some form of assistance.

STAKING

The most natural way of supporting any plant is to use sticks of some sort. In the wild, plants in need of support are likely to scramble up through other plants, shrubs in particular, and so using twigs is simply a way of copying this. Hazel twigs, which are commonly used as pea-sticks, are the best. Push these into the ground around the plants, bending over the tops at about half to two-thirds of the eventual height of the plants. The plants will then grow up through the twigs, completely hiding them but deriving support from them.

A similar low-tech staking method is to place a series of canes in the ground around the edges of the clump and weave a cat's cradle of string between them. The plants will grow up through the strings, gaining support from but hiding the framework.

Garden suppliers produce supports in metal and plastic. These consist of stakes with a hoop at the top, sometimes with cross-bars to form a mesh, or inverted L-shaped pieces of wire which interlock. A do-it-yourself version of this is useful for large areas of tall annuals. Suspend a section of wide-mesh wire netting horizontally between four or more stakes. The plants grow up through the gaps in the netting, obtaining perfect support. It is equally possible to do this with plastic netting.

PROTECTING PLANTS

It is often necessary to protect plants from mammals and birds, especially at the early stages of growth when plants are succulent and at their most vulnerable. The simplest way is to drop wire netting cages over the plants. These may look ugly but they are very effective and can be removed once the plants are less attractive to their enemies. They can also be left in place as supports for the plants to grow through. A low hedge of box may be grown around the bed, although this would take several years to reach the required density and might not be enough to deter mammals. Alternatively, a low fence of wire netting can be placed around the bed, but this is not very attractive.

Plants may need protecting from wind and frost. The former can be countered by creating a wind-break. In the long term this could be a hedge, but plastic netting can be used as a temporary expedient. Tender annuals should not be planted out too early, but if a rogue frost is expected, cover the plants with horticultural fleece or newspaper. Cloches give longer term protection should it be needed.

A SELECTION OF STAKING METHODS

1 A mesh, here a proprietary hoop made of galvanized steel, can be placed over the emerging plants to give them support. As they grow, the stems pass through the mesh, which gives the support, and their foliage will hide the mesh.

2 Proprietary linking stakes can be erected around and through the middle of a group of plants. They can be used on any size or shape of clump, and can also be used to restore a clump of plants after they have collapsed.

3 Give support to a large area of plants by fixing a section of large-meshed wire netting above them on short stakes. The netting will soon be hidden as the plants grow through it, gaining support from the many cross-wires.

MAKING A CAT'S CRADLE

1 A cat's-cradle made of garden string makes a good temporary support. Push a few canes into the ground around and in the middle of the plants. To avoid eye injuries, trim the canes down to just above the height of where you intend to tie the string.

2 Tie garden string between the canes in a random pattern to create a network of cross-strings. They can be wrapped round the posts and only tied every so often just to keep the string taut.

3 The plants will grow through the cat's-cradle, deriving flexible support from the strings. Discard the string at the end of the season along with the plants.

USING PEA-STICKS

1 A network of fine sticks or twigs can be erected around and over a plant clump of any size, so that their stems will be supported as they grow. Push the sticks into the ground around the clump.

2 Bend over and weave or tie their tops together to create a network through which the stems will grow. The sticks will need renewing each year.

Above: *Tall single-stemmed plants like this foxglove can be staked with a single cane. Push firmly into the ground and attach with one or more plant ties. Canes are dangerous, so put a cap on it so that no one gets poked in the eye.*

Weed Control

One of the least attractive chores associated with any garden plant is keeping it free of weeds. This is no less a chore with annuals, but as long as you keep on top of it, weeding can be a relaxing pastime. While weeding you are closer to the plants than you would be simply strolling past, so it is hardly surprising that this is when you will often notice detail in the flowers that you would normally miss. It also gives you the opportunity to check that each plant is healthy and not suffering from any pest or disease.

WEEDING

The secret of successful weeding is thorough ground preparation before you sow or plant and then to keep on top of the weeding by doing it regularly. Once you lose control of the weeds in a bed, they begin to take over, after which weeding becomes an uphill battle.

Never plant a bed that has weeds already in it. Clean it thoroughly first. Once you have planted, hoe between the plants regularly to kill any newly germinated weeds. Once the plants begin to fill out, hoeing will be less easy so you will have to resort to hand-weeding. However, by this stage there should be few weeds and it is more a matter of keeping an eye out for the odd weed and pulling it out before it can become too large or start spreading.

MULCHES

You can cut down considerably on the labour of weeding by preventing weed seeds from germinating, and a mulch is an effective way to achieve this, though it will not stop perennial weeds. A mulch is a layer of well-rotted organic material, chipped bark or a similar material, which is placed on the surface of the soil. When applying a mulch, always water first, then cover the soil with a 10cm (4in) layer.

Peat does not have much value as a mulch because it will blow away as soon as it dries out and it adds very little to the soil as it breaks down. Straw and grass cuttings can be used but they are extremely ugly and are best reserved for the back of beds where they are hidden from view by tall plants. Farmyard manure is good but quality varies and frequently it is full of weed seed just waiting to germinate.

HERBICIDES

Try to avoid using too many chemicals in the garden. It may be necessary, especially on heavy soils, to use herbicides to clear the ground initially, but after planting they are best avoided, as they are likely to damage adjacent plants.

EFFECTIVE WEEDING

1 Weeds should be eradicated for several reasons: they make a bed look untidy; they use up a great deal of moisture and nutrients; many harbour pests and diseases.

2 Where plants are close together, the best way of removing weeds is to either pull them out by hand or dig them out using a hand fork. Perennial weeds must be dug out whole and not simply chopped off, or they will soon return.

MULCHES

Black polythene (plastic) *Good but unattractive*
Chipped or composted bark *Excellent*
Farmyard manure *Moderate*
Garden compost *Good*
Grass cuttings *Good but unattractive*
Gravel *Good*
Leaf mould *Excellent*
Peat *Poor*
Spent hops *Good*
Spent mushroom compost *Good but alkaline*
Straw *Good but unattractive*

3 Where there is more room, hoes can be used in a border, but take care to avoid your precious plants. In hot weather hoed-up weeds can be left to shrivel, but it looks much neater if they are all removed to the compost heap.

4 After weeding, rake through the border with a fork, or if the plants are far enough apart with a rake. This will tidy up the bed and level off the surface, removing any footprints and any weed remnants.

Below: *This well-tended border is an excellent example of one in which the weeds are kept at bay partly by weeding and partly by close planting. This technique means that the weeds cannot become established.*

5 It is a good idea to apply or renew a mulch after weeding. As well as helping to prevent weeds from reappearing, this will also preserve moisture. Composted or chipped bark will set the plants off well.

Dealing with Pests and Diseases

Pests and diseases are perhaps what gardeners detest most about gardening. Fortunately, annuals are less prone to these annoyances than many other plants, but if they do succumb it does not really matter. You can simply dig them up, throw them away and start again with little financial loss, something that you would be loath to do with an expensive tree or shrub.

PREVENTION
One way of avoiding problems with pests and diseases is to take preventative action right from the start. Choose only healthy, pest-free plants. Avoid buying or using anything about which you are doubtful. Even if a plant does not look diseased but just thin and weak, reject it as it is far more likely to be disease-prone than a healthy one. Next, prepare your ground thoroughly, removing any weeds, some of which may act as carriers of disease, especially fungal diseases such as rusts. An additional advantage of thoroughly preparing the ground is that it will help produce strong, vigorous plants, which are far less likely to succumb to disease.

Another way of avoiding problems is to have a mixed garden. Monocultures are far more open to destructive attacks than ones that contain a very wide range of plants. Old-fashioned cottage gardens survived without the armoury of chemicals that we now have for this very reason. They grew a wide diversity of plants, some of which harboured predators that reduced pest populations. Pests and diseases are often plant specific and so a wide spectrum of plants means that the problems have less chance of becoming established and sweeping through the whole garden. So, as well as growing annuals also grow plenty of perennials, shrubs and trees. Shrubs attract birds, which often help to keep pest populations under control.

DISPOSING OF PLANTS
If problems do occur there are several ways of coping with them. The first may seem extreme but it quickly solves the problem. Destroy the infected plants. Annuals can be replaced easily, even if you have to wait until the next year. Once they become infected, even if you use a chemical treatment, they may not have enough reserves, unlike perennials, to recover properly and will put on a poor show.

PHYSICAL MEANS
The second approach is to physically remove the problem. Slugs and snails, for example, can be treated with chemicals but their populations can be reduced to acceptable levels by going out after dark (when they are at their most active) with a torch and picking them up. Rabbits and other mammals can be kept at bay with fences or similar methods of protection. Even aphids can be removed by hand as long as the infestation is not great and if you do not mind doing it.

CHEMICALS
The third, and many consider to be the least acceptable, method of control is to use chemicals in the form of sprays or powders. Always follow the manufacturer's instructions with regard to their use, dosage and any protective clothing that you should wear. Specific pesticides and fungicides are frequently changing and it is best that you get local advice from your garden centre or nursery as to what to use to treat any problems that arise. When using chemicals, spray only the infected area, do not drench every plant in sight.

Above: *Some of the methods used to combat pests. These include netting and black thread to keep off or deter birds and mammals, baits for slugs and snails, puffer packs of chemical dust as well as liquid sprays for insect pests and fungal diseases.*

Left: *Rabbits and other mammals are likely to chew the plants right down to the ground and should be kept at bay with wire-netting fences.*

Above: *This plant shows the typical results of browsing by slugs and snails. All the succulent flowers, leaves and stems are likely to be eaten. Slug bait or picking them off by hand are the most effective methods of protection.*

Above: *The caterpillars of butterflies and moths eat leaves, at best leaving holes in flowers and leaves and at worst eating them completely. Picking off the eggs or caterpillars by hand is the best means of defence, although chemicals can be used.*

Above: *Aphids are the most common of airborne pests. Here, aphids congregate to sap the juices of a leaf, and they will also attack buds, flowers and even succulent stems. Encouraging ladybirds and other predators is the best means of defence, but chemicals can be used as a last resort.*

Above: *Fungal diseases, such as rusts or this mildew, can be a problem, especially in either wet or very dry years. Plenty of air circulating round the plants is a great aid to prevention. Plants subjected to bad fungal attacks are best removed and burnt. The effort to cure the problem on annuals is not worth it.*

INDEX

ACKNOWLEDGEMENTS

The publishers would like to thank the following for their permission to photograph their plants and gardens for this book:
Hilary and Richard Bird; the RHS Garden, Wisley; Mavis and David Seeney; and Merriments Gardens, Kent.

The publishers would also like to thank the following picture agencies for allowing their pictures to be reproduced in this book:

The Garden Picture Library for the pictures on pages 2tl (John Neubauer), 2tr (John Glover), 2bl (Steven Wooster), 2br (Steven Wooster), 3 (Howard Rice), 4 (Steven Wooster), 5 (Vaughan Fleming), 11tl (Steven Wooster), 11bl (Jerry Pavia), 11r (Sunniva Harte), 13t (Howard Rice), 14b (John Neubauer), 15tl (Eric Crichton), 15bl (Howard Rice), 15r (John Glover), 17br (John Glover), 17bl (Gary Rogers), 18b (Steven Wooster), 19bl (JS Sira), 19br (David Askham), 22 (Eric Crichton), 23l (Lamontagne), 23r (Steven Wooster), 29bl (John Glover), 38 (A. I. Lord), 39tl (Lamontagne), 39bl (Vaughan Fleming), 39r (Howard Rice), 40 (Kathy Charlton), 41tl (Vaughan Fleming), 41bl (Chris Burrows), 41r (Howard Rice), 61bl (Jerry Pavia), 61r (Howard Rice), 67br (John Glover), 68t (Brian Carter), 68b (John Glover), 71br (JS Sira), 77r (Friedrich Strauss), 82 (Brigitte Thomas), 91br (Lamontagne), 94t (Vaughan Fleming), 94b (John Glover), 95t (Kathy Charlton), 95b (Lamontagne) and 96 (Howard Rice).
Andrew Lawson Photography for the front cover image.